HO'OPONOPONO

HO'OPONOPONO

Contemporary Uses of a Hawaiian Problem-Solving Process

E. VICTORIA SHOOK

An East-West Center Book
from the Institute of Culture and Communication
Published for the East-West Center
by the University of Hawaii Press

© 1985 by The East-West Center
All rights reserved
Library of Congress Catalog Card Number 85–51886
ISBN 0–8248–1047–3
Manufactured in the United States of America

To my father and mother

Contents

Preface

Every book is a destination of sorts, and once in a while I find myself both amused and surprised to think of the road that led me here. As is also the case when looking back, I realize how many fortunate circumstances and people have lent support to my efforts. I want to acknowledge these events and people here.

First, the events. . . . In the spring of 1978 I was a high school teacher and drug education coordinator in Guam. Along with a small group of educators I visited Hawaii to observe drug education programs. Our purpose was to garner whatever insights we could to assist in curriculum development appropriate for Guam's multicultural community. During the trip I met a woman who gave me her personal copy of *Nānā I Ke Kumu*, a book of Hawaiian mental health practices that had descriptions and anecdotes about a problem-solving process called *ho'oponopono*. As were others in my group who read the description, I was struck by the simple elegance and common-sense ideas of the process. Although thoroughly Hawaiian, *ho'oponopono* seemed to express many of the underlying values and beliefs that were also prevalent on Guam in the Chamorro culture. We returned to Guam invigorated and began our curriculum project with a few ideas on how to make it more Pacific-oriented.

After an exciting and successful year of developing and testing our pilot drug education program, I still had some doubts about how successful we had been in making it truly appropriate for use in Guam. Had we simply taken a mainland program and dressed it up in culture-garb? It seemed as if much more needed to be done, but I did not know exactly what it was. Graduate school at the University of Hawaii seemed a likely place to investigate the issues.

During the next two years I focused my studies on cross-cultural com-

munication and mental health and followed up on my interest in
ho'oponopono. Eventually this led to a research project on current
ho'oponopono uses and a technical report on the subject (Shook 1981).
The report was supported, printed, and distributed by the Sub-Regional
Child Welfare Training Center of the School of Social Work at the University of Hawaii-Manoa and by the Region 9 Child Abuse and Neglect
Resource Center. Later, a committee at the East-West Center recommended the manuscript for publication by the center. With this encouragement and interest I revised and expanded the 1981 report.

My acknowledgments now must shift from the circumstantial events
to the individuals who contributed so much to my efforts. My deepest
respect and gratitude for their generosity and patience goes to the individuals I interviewed. This book is, after all, their story. Many others
have enriched this work, and although I thank them all, there are a few I
wish to single out: Joyce Winn for her gift of *Nānā I Ke Kumu* and her
great enthusiasm; Lynette Paglinawan for her faith, guidance, and teaching; Richard Brislin and Geoffrey White for their critical analyses and
suggestions on content and organization; Walter Lonner for relaying to
the East-West Center some beneficial improvements needed in the draft;
and to the East-West Center editor, Tina Clark, for valuable changes that
helped to smooth and polish the manuscript. Finally, I thank my friends
Jay Ercanbrack, Michele Hill, Peggy Givins, and my husband John
Seniuk, who all, in one way or another, provided me with unfailing
moral support, inspiration, and love.

January 1985

Honolulu, Hawaii

CHAPTER 1

An Introduction to the
Practice of Ho'oponopono

A rich body of knowledge about the physical, emotional, and spiritual well-being of an individual in relationship to family, community, and environment has existed in the Hawaiian culture for centuries. One of the specific practices is a complex system for maintaining harmonious relationships and resolving conflict within the extended family; this system is called *ho'oponopono* (pronounced, hō'ō pōnō pōnō), which means "setting to right." Within the last ten years this concept has become popularized and a number of individuals, mostly within social service programs, have attempted to use this traditional family concept and practice. The purpose of this study is to illustrate how some individuals on the island of Oahu have adapted *ho'oponopono* for use in their social service agencies or private consultation and counseling practices.

It is likely that many variations exist in the description and practice of *ho'oponopono*. The description that has received the most widespread acknowledgment is that given by Mary Kawena Pukui, a respected *kumu* (teacher) of Hawaiian culture, to the Culture Committee of the Queen Liliuokalani Children's Center in Honolulu. Details of how this knowledge was transmitted are included in this chapter. As stated in the preface of *Nānā I Ke Kumu,* which means "look to the source," Pukui was the ideal *kumu* (Pukui, Haertig, and Lee 1972).[1]

All the individuals in the present study drew on the basic explanation of *ho'oponopono* as given by Pukui. Therefore it is possible to trace a process of diffusion for that particular strain of *ho'oponopono*. The major portion of this work is devoted to describing variations in recent *ho'oponopono* use by social service providers. In addition, two individuals who are trained as social workers and who have the most extensive experience using the process shared an outline of their model of *ho'o-ponopono*, which appears in a later chapter.

The practice of *ho'oponopono* is best understood by first appreciating the Hawaiian historic and cultural context in which it is embedded. The second section of this chapter is devoted to this aim. For readers who are interested in *ho'oponopono*'s relationship to issues in cross-cultural mental health, chapter 2 will provide such a perspective. Individual case studies are presented in chapter 3 followed by chapter 4's detailed exploration of the variations. The final chapter examines conclusions that may be drawn and suggests implications for further study.

THE CULTURAL CONTEXT FOR HO'OPONOPONO

To understand the significance of the current use of *ho'oponopono* on Oahu, it is necessary to see how it is related to both traditional and modern features of the Hawaiian culture. The reader will gain background information that is both cross-cultural and culture-specific and relates to an analytic framework frequently referred to as "emics" and "etics." The terms, borrowed from linguistics (phonemic and phonetic), have become familiar parlance in anthropology and other cross-cultural disciplines.[2] Emic refers to the within-culture point of view, while etic refers to generalized constructs that can be used across cultures. For example, an etic category might be called "conflict resolution strategies" with *ho'oponopono* as an emic construct. Any attempt at understanding the place of *ho'oponopono* within the Hawaiian-American cultural matrix must begin with describing some salient characteristics of "Hawaiian-ness." Although full treatment of this topic is beyond the scope of this work, it is possible to glean from available sources a configuration of values and practices, particularly about family and child rearing, that suggest complementarity with *ho'oponopono*.[3] Contrary to many other Hawaiian practices such as *hula* (dance), *lū'au* (feast), *hānai* (adoption), and other features that have had continuous use, the present use of *ho'oponopono* as described here is a result of specific attempts during the last 20 years to revive it for social work practice.[4] A brief reconstruction of the events that culminated in the reemergence of *ho'oponopono* is presented here, as well as a basic definition and description of the version of *ho'oponopono* that evolved during the process.

Defining Hawaiian

In a multicultural society like Hawaii, there has been confusion over how to establish ethnic and cultural boundaries. How can "Hawaiian" be defined for this study? In 1983 the number of pure Hawaiians was estimated to be quite low at 8,291. The number of part-Hawaiians was much higher at 174,579, which totals approximately 19 percent of the state's population.[5] Numerous problems exist in determining the prime cultural affiliation of individuals with mixed ancestry, and there is disagreement among agencies in Hawaii on how ethnicity should be determined.[6] In his book on Hawaiian-American coping strategies, Howard (1974, 91) presented a useful distinction between ethnic and cultural variables.

> "Ethnic" patterns may be conceptually distinguished from "cultural" patterns; the former are perpetuated by reinforcements given to them by persons external to the group, or category, while the latter, once learned, are self-sustaining. Thus, on one hand, a person may be legally defined as a Hawaiian even though he was raised by a Caucasian (or Filipino, or Chinese) family without ever having been exposed to Hawaiian cultural heritage. . . . On the other hand, an individual raised as a Hawaiian may be strongly influenced by Hawaiian cultural traditions even though ethnically defined as a haole or Japanese.

Howard's study cites works that focus on a Hawaiian cultural pattern which may, therefore, include beliefs, values, and practices of persons of various ethnicities. In the works on Hawaiians, however, it is assumed that the majority are ethnically at least part-Hawaiian.

Much of the traditional Hawaiian culture has been left behind and cannot be considered a defining feature of contemporary Hawaiian identity. These remnants from the past include a hierarchical social organization, traditional land-use patterns, and the material culture of precontact Hawaii, which has been relegated largely to museum exhibits. Knowledge of traditional folk medicine, which seems to be held primarily by the elder members of the community, is another measure of Hawaiian identification (Howard 1974). Today, the elders' knowledge and skills are being supplanted by Western ones as exposure to American ideas and practices becomes widespread. The use of the Hawaiian language as a vehicle for transmitting culture from one generation to the next has diminished greatly. It is estimated that only approximately 2,000 native Hawaiian speakers remain, and these individuals are more than 60 years old.[7]

What then is left? Despite the dramatic loss of the social organization of the *ali'i* (chief) system, the language, the land, and many cultural traditions, there seems to be a recognizable pattern of social interaction identified as Hawaiian or perhaps more accurately as Hawaiian-American. Some of the prominent features include the periodic use of Hawaiian words and phrases, the use of a Hawaiian-Creole language called "pidgin,"[8] and a style of speech called "talk story," which is defined by Boggs, Watson-Gegeo, and McMillan (1985).

> Talk story is a complex art consisting of recalled personal events, parts of legends, joking, verbal play and ordinary conversation. According to one

local observer, people often talk story as a means of searching for and recognizing shared feelings.

The continued importance of music, dancing, and singing at social gatherings is often noted as a Hawaiian pattern. Recently, Hawaiian organizations and various educational institutions have increased their efforts to revive and strengthen cultural traditions, including language, traditional music and dance forms, mythology, and the environmental knowledge that guided early Hawaiians. In some cases, the groups are attempting to apply this knowledge in ways that significantly change their lifestyles. Perhaps the feature of cultural identity that is most central to my study is the continued preference by Hawaiians of employing a social interaction style that stresses interpersonal harmony and avoidance of overt conflict.

If we examine both the meaning of the Hawaiian family and the beliefs and practices that constitute a system of social order, we can see how this complementary emphasis on maintaining harmony and avoiding conflict operates. Once this foundation is laid, ho'oponopono as a conflict resolution method begins to rest securely.

Family and Socialization

The extended family in Hawaiian culture is the center of life. The word for family, 'ohana, is derived from the words 'oha, for taro, and na, the designation for plural. The taro plant is linked with myths about the origin of people, as well as being the staple food. The meaning of 'ohana, therefore, takes on metaphorical significance. Pukui stated, "members of the 'ohana, like taro shoots, are all from the root" (Pukui, Haertig, and Lee 1972, 166). Pukui explained that 'ohana is also:

> . . . sense of unity, shared involvement and shared responsibility. It is mutual interdependence and mutual help. It is emotional support given and received. It is solidarity and cohesiveness. It is love—often; it is loyalty—always. It is all this, encompassed by the joined links of blood relationship. (Pukui, Haertig, and Lee 1972, 171)

Children have an important role in the family and are desired by most adults. Hānai, or adoption, is a frequent practice. In a study of a Hawaiian Homelands community on the leeward coast of Oahu, Gallimore, Boggs, and Jordan (1974) reported that 30 percent of the families had children other than their own living in the house. The authors also listed two common reasons given by informants for taking a child in a hānai relationship: (1) a woman is unable to bear a child, or (2) a woman with older children desires an infant. Infants are generally indulged and are often the focus of attention in the family. Because of this value and the practice of *hānai*, high rates of illegitimacy are not an overbearing cause for concern in the Hawaiian community. Once children are brought into the world, they are to be cared for and loved (Young 1980).

As an infant becomes a toddler, a shift in attention occurs. The child is no longer indulged and is expected to begin assuming family responsibilities. Older siblings are involved in caring for the younger children. Thus the child-rearing process fosters interdependence and increased opportunity to exercise adult-type roles by working and contributing to the family's economic and social welfare.

The family's structure is characterized by what might be called a benevolent authoritarianism. Elders, the *kūpuna*, are respected for their wisdom and experience and are often the teachers of the children. Two phrases illustrate the revered place of *kūpuna* in the family.

• *Oi ka 'aka 'a na maka* (while the eyes are still open) admonishes young people to learn from the old people while they are still alive—"eyes still open."

• *Make no ke kalo a ola i ka* means the taro may die but it lives on in its young offshoots (Handy and Pukui 1972, 179–180).

Children learn household tasks through observation and experience. They learn to be unobtrusive since to do otherwise is to risk rebuff and punishment. They may seek help and approval from adults, but in a subtle manner that is not intrusive. Rewards and punishments in the family are often meted out to a group rather than to an individual. This fosters what Gallimore, Boggs, and Jordan (1974) have named as one of the two primary strategies used by children to get along in the family: sibling cooperation. The other strategy is conflict avoidance with adults.

All these socialization practices underscore a predominant value pattern of affiliation. This value is expressed often in the Hawaiian language with words such as *laulima* (cooperation) and *kōkua* (help), words that reinforce the idea of cooperation and interdependence. Generosity, hospitality, sharing, and reciprocity are also valued. These values have application to many areas of endeavor, including work. For example, *ukupau* is still used by some businesses in Hawaii. The word refers to the practice of people helping one another with their work tasks so that they can finish early and commence with fun and relaxation. This contrasts with the predominant American work pattern of adhering to a strict time clock system and requiring workers to be on the job for a specified period of time regardless of task completion. Another example illustrating these Hawaiian values is the work involved in a party, or *lū'au*. Preparation of the many varieties and large quantities of food for a *lū'au* requires that many people contribute time, money, and skill. With the spirit of *laulima,* however, this cooperative work has its own reward in the pleasant social interaction and accomplishment of what otherwise might be a formidable task.

The successful maturation of a person in the Hawaiian culture thus requires that an individual cultivate an accurate ability to perceive and attend to other people's needs, often without being asked. These are attitudes and behaviors that help cement the relationships of the *'ohana* and the community.

Social Order

A philosophical look at Hawaiian concepts unearths a profound belief in a universe that operates on principles of harmonious relationships. Mossman and Wahilani (1975) explain:

> There is a natural and harmonious order to the entire universe. The three major forces are the God(s), nature and man. The Hawaiian of old realized that it was necessary that these forces be kept in "harmony" and that they were all in some way interrelated.

Evidence of the importance of this triad of relationships can be seen in the social values and beliefs that affect the selection of practices used to maintain social order.

First, spiritual concerns pervade much of Hawaiian interaction and ceremony. The recent popularity of traditional forms of *hula* has brought back a strong spiritual element to dance. Blessings of work endeavors, social gatherings, and opening and closing ceremonies are commonplace. Paglinawan (1980) and Mossman and Wahilani assert that Christian values coexist with a deep respect for the ancient gods.

The love of nature is also apparent in the popular phrase *aloha 'āina* (love of the land). There has been a resurgence of Makahiki festivals in recent years. These yearly celebrations, traditionally held in the fall, were a time for sports and religious activities and were a tribute to Lono, the Hawaiian god of agriculture. Today's festivities usually combine the spiritual tribute with an opportunity to build community strength and conduct community fundraising activities. Another example of the eminence of land can be found in the focus of an activist group called the *'Ohana.* The group is dedicated to the protection of an uninhabited island, Kaho'olawe, used as a bombing target by the U.S. military. Members and supporters of the *'Ohana* maintain that Kaho'olawe has significant historic and spiritual value and should be treated with due respect. A final example supporting the centrality of nature in Hawaiian experience is the state motto: *Ua mau ke ea o ka 'āina i ka pono* (the life of the land is preserved in righteousness).

Perhaps the importance of harmony in relationships can best be summed up by the attributes of the word *aloha*. This often-used Hawaiian word expresses love and also is a greeting and a farewell. More subtly, it suggests the highly valued character traits of generosity, friendliness, patience, and productivity. The spirit of *aloha* carries with it an understanding that the ability to soothe and prevent conflicts, shame, and other disruptive occurrences is important, and that if the harmony has been disrupted, one should have the courage to ask for and give forgiveness.

A fascinating study of how some of these facets of Hawaiian philosophy manifest themselves in the ideology and behavior of contemporary Hawaiians was done by Ito (1978). Her anthropological study of urban Hawaiian women elaborated on a concept she termed "retributive comeback." She suggested that the women studied believed that negative sanctions, such as illness or misfortune, would befall them or their kin if they acted, felt, or thought in a negative way toward another person. Negative relationships with others created entanglements called *hihia*. In order to ameliorate this negative state of affairs, the individuals were required to restore balance and harmony through self-scrutiny, admitting their wrongdoing, asking forgiveness, and making restitution where possible. If an individual was unable to ask forgiveness, then changing one's behavior or enlisting the help of a spiritual ally such as the Christian God or a family *'aumakua* (ancestor god) could suffice. This is an example of how the belief in the interrelatedness of kin, ancestors, and the natural world manifests itself. The belief in retribution, with its remedy of self-scrutiny, confession, and forgiveness, is strikingly similar to the underlying beliefs and overt practices in *ho'oponopono*. Perhaps the presence of the "symbolic conscience," as Ito calls it, in contemporary Hawaiians is one thing that makes *ho'oponopono* a timely and functional remedy for Hawaiians today.[9]

THE REEMERGENCE OF HO'OPONOPONO

Although variations of *ho'oponopono* had been in existence before the Europeans came to Hawaii, the practice had fallen from popular use quite dramatically by the mid-1900s. Those elements of the process that were influenced by Hawaiian religious practices and beliefs were most subject to abandonment. Some of the remaining modifications of *ho'oponopono* retained the essential purpose of problem solving but were greatly simplified. One such practice that incorporated Christian values was opening the Bible and pointing to a passage that might give insight and guidance to a troubled individual or group. *Ho'oponopono* could also mean getting together with family members to talk out problems or to seek forgiveness for a transgression. It was not until the publication of *Nānā I Ke Kumu* in 1972 that a detailed description of one style of *ho'oponopono,* with case examples, was available to the general public.

The story that follows reconstructs a fascinating odyssey of questioning and sharing among a group of social workers, a Hawaiiana expert, and a psychiatrist that eventually led to the transformation of *ho'oponopono* from a little-known and little-understood practice to one that is now familiar, at least in concept, to many. The story also illustrates how one social worker, who also appears later in the case studies, learned to utilize cultural issues in a counseling situation, greatly enhancing his ability to assist a Hawaiian family.

In 1963, a young social worker who worked at the Queen Liliuokalani Children's Center (QLCC) was given a case involving a seriously delinquent boy and his mother.[10] Previously this case had been handled by seven agencies. It was a difficult case because it involved cultural issues that earlier case workers had been unable to understand and resolve. Keola Espiritu (pseudonym), the young social worker, had been given the case by the QLCC director because of Keola's interest in Hawaiiana.

While uncovering the details of the problem, Keola learned that the mother attributed the cause of the boy's problems to a curse that had affected him since his birth. The curse was the result of a promise the woman had made to her dying mother—a promise that later had been broken. The woman had promised never to marry a divorced person and eventually had done so.

The repercussions of this broken promise were realized shortly after her son's birth. When the baby was born, he was unnaturally still, not crying or moving. The mother fasted *(ho'okeai)* in order to divine the nature of the problem. During the fast she had an insight that linked the baby's lack of movement to her broken promise. After her realization the baby began to respond more normally. Some years later the father died, leaving his wife and son alone. The son had gotten into trouble as an adolescent and by the time the case was at QLCC, Keola reported that he thought the boy was "flirting with death," because of two serious encounters with the police. In one incident the boy pulled an unloaded .45-caliber pistol on a police officer; in another he challenged 15 officers to a karate duel.

The case presented quite a dilemma for the social worker who, although raised in rural Oahu with strong Hawaiian traditions, had received professional training with a Western cultural orientation:

How the hell am I gonna' deal with this kind of cultural stuff? If you ask me as a native Hawaiian, I would know—I would run to a grandparent or somebody for help.

When Keola shared this concern with his supervisor he was given permission to contact Mary Kawena Pukui (also called Tūtū, an affectionate and respectful name for an older person that loosely means "grandma" or "grandpa"). He approached Tūtū Pukui and requested her assistance so that the agency could learn how to help this and other Hawaiian families "the Hawaiian way."

Tūtū consented; she, a psychiatrist, a psychologist, and several social workers began meeting on a weekly basis as the "Culture Committee." Consultation with a psychiatrist/psychologist team was an established part of social work practice at that time, but the addition of a cultural resource person was a unique departure, particularly in the early 1960s.

The process that Keola and the others used to articulate the cultural concepts was not a didactic one. Instead, case material was brought to the committee, then Tūtū would "talk story" about related beliefs and practices. The sessions were taped for reference. The committee participants learned that the key to understanding a concept's complexity and depth of meaning was to ask questions about it in many different ways. Through this method Keola and the others explored the concepts that were pertinent to his case; these included 'ohana, ho'okeai, ho'ohiki (promises), the consequences of breaking promises, and the methods for resolving problems. The subject of ho'oponopono came to light when the group discussed traditional remedies for family problems.

Tūtū talked about a form of ho'oponopono that she had used all her life and that had been used by her family in Ka'u, Hawaii. It was an understanding of ho'oponopono based on practical experience.

I took part in ho'oponopono myself for 47 years, from semi-Christian to Christian times. And whether my 'ohana [family] prayed to 'aumākua [ancestor gods] or to God, the whole idea of ho'oponopono was the same. Everyone of us searched his heart for hard feelings against one another. Before God and with His help, we forgave and were forgiven, thrashing out every grudge, peeve, or resentment among us. (Pukui, Haertig, and Lee 1972, 61)

During the Culture Committee meetings, as specific concepts of ho'oponopono were explored by examining situations that Pukui and others presented, it was possible to draw parallels to Western concepts and practices. The psychiatrist, Dr. Haertig, made invaluable contributions in this area.

It was Pukui's method that Keola used with the woman and her son to help them understand and resolve their problems, untangling the mixture of Hawaiian and Christian beliefs that had confounded the issues. The intervention resulted in a positive outcome. According to Keola, the boy was able to finish high school and "make it in society."

The excitement generated by the possibility of similar beneficial outcomes in other cases, as well as the amount of learning that was taking place as a result of the weekly meetings, kept the group going for seven years. The QLCC staff realized that sensitizing workers to cultural beliefs and practices should be a primary goal of their work, particularly since QLCC was an agency serving the Hawaiian community. Since a voluminous amount of material from the committee's work had been collected during the years, QLCC decided to publish a book. *Nānā I Ke Kumu* was designed to be a "source book of Hawaiian cultural practices, concepts and beliefs which illustrates the wisdom and dignity contained in the cultural roots of every Hawaiian child" (Pukui, Haertig, and Lee 1972, vii). Volume 1, published in 1972, concentrated on defining and giving examples of specific customs, while volume 2, published in 1979, articulated larger patterns of beliefs and concepts with particular emphasis on basic emotions.

In a related project, some years after the committee began, QLCC tested the practice of *ho'oponopono* in the social work setting. A Hawaiian social worker was hired to do a one-year research project involving the use of *ho'oponopono* with Hawaiian families. The results of the project, *Ho'oponopono Project II* (Paglinawan 1972), were published and gave details on the cases of three families. During this project the author further refined and articulated the problem-solving process and clarified issues that needed further study.[11]

The description of *ho'oponopono* that follows is based primarily on these two sources of information: *Nānā I Ke Kumu* (Volume 1) and *Ho'oponopono Project II*. This is the same resource material that was potentially available to the individuals in this study who used *ho'oponopono*. All interviewed persons acknowledged *Nānā I Ke Kumu* as a primary source on the subject.

A DESCRIPTION

Ho'oponopono is a method for restoring harmony that was traditionally used within the extended family. According to Pukui, it literally means "setting to right . . . to restore and maintain good relationships among family, and family and supernatural powers" (1972, 60).[12] The metaphor of a tangled net has been used to illustrate how problems within a family affect not only persons directly involved but also other family members. The family is a complex net of relationships, and any disturbance in one part of the net will pull other parts. This metaphor reinforces the Hawaiian philosophy of the interrelatedness of all things.

The family conference was traditionally led by a senior family member or, if necessary, by a respected outsider such as a *kahuna lapa'au* (healer). The problem-solving process is a complex and potentially lengthy one that includes prayer, statement of the problem, discussion, confession of wrongdoing, restitution when necessary, forgiveness, and release. An outline of the conditions and steps of *ho'oponopono* and an abbreviated example of a hypothetical *ho'oponopono* session follow.

The Steps

Ho'oponopono is opened with *pule,* which is prayer conducted to ask God and/or the *'aumakua* for assistance and blessing in the problem-solving endeavor. *Pule* is usually led by the senior person conducting the session. Reliance on spiritual assistance heightens and strengthens the emotional commitment of the participants. Prayer lays the foundation for sincerity and truthfulness, necessary conditions to be maintained throughout the process.

In the beginning phase there is a period of identifying the general problem, known as *kūkulu kumuhana.* (This term has two additional meanings that are a part of *ho'oponopono. Kūkulu kumuhana* is the pooling of strengths for a shared purpose, such as solving the family's problem. It also refers to the leader's effort to reach out to a person who is resisting the *ho'oponopono* process to enable that person to participate fully.) During this initial phase the procedures for the whole problem-solving sequence are also outlined in order to reacquaint all participants with them.

Once the proper climate is set, the leader focuses on the specific problem. The *hala,* or transgression, is stated. *Hala* also implies that the perpetrator and the person wronged are bound together in a relationship of negative entanglement called *hihia.*

Because of the nature of *hihia,* most problems have many dimensions. The initial hurt is often followed by other reactions, further misunderstandings, and so forth until a complex knot of difficulties has evolved. It is the leader's responsibility to choose one of the problems and work it out with the family through the process of *mahiki,* or discussion. With one part resolved, the group can uncover and resolve successive layers of trouble one layer at a time until the family relationships are again free and clear.

The discussion of the problem is led and channeled by the leader. This intermediary function keeps individuals from directly confronting one another, a situation that could lead to further emotional outburst and misunderstanding. Traditionally, the Hawaiians felt that allowing emotional expressions to escalate discouraged problem resolution. Each participant who has been affected by the problem in some way—directly or indirectly—is asked to share his or her feelings, or *mana'o*. The emphasis is on self-scrutiny, and when participants share they are encouraged to do so honestly, openly, and in a way that avoids blame and recrimination. If in the course of the discussion tempers begin to flare, the leader may declare *ho'omalu,* a cooling-off period of silence. This enables the family to reflect once again on the purpose of the process and to bring their aroused emotions under control.

When the discussion is complete, the *mihi* takes place. This is the sincere confession of wrongdoing and the seeking of forgiveness. It is expected that forgiveness be given whenever asked.[13] If restitution is necessary then the terms of it are arranged and agreed upon.

Closely related to *mihi* is *kala,* or a loosening of the negative entanglements. Both the person who has confessed and the person who has forgiven are expected to *kala* the problem. This mutual release is an essential part of the process and true *ho'oponopono* is not complete without it. The *kala* indicates that the conflicts and hurts have been released and are *oki* (cut off).

The *pani* is the closing phase and may include a summary of what has taken place and, importantly, a reaffirmation of the family's strengths and enduring bonds. The problem that has been worked out is declared closed, never to be brought up again. If other layers of the problem need to be worked out, the final *pani* is postponed. Sometimes *ho'oponopono* may take many sessions. Each session has a *pani* about what has been resolved and includes a closing prayer, *pule ho'opau.* After the session the family and leader traditionally share a snack or meal to which all have contributed. This demonstrates the commitment and bond of all who participated and provides a familiar means to move from the formal problem-solving setting to normal daily routines.

In summary, *ho'oponopono* is a highly structured process with four distinct phases: an opening phase that includes the prayer and a statement of the problem; a discussion phase in which all members involved share their thoughts and feelings in a calm manner and listen to all the others as they speak; a resolution phase that enables the exchange of confession, forgiveness, and release; and a closing phase to summarize what has transpired and to give spiritual and individual thanks for sincere participation.

The following example of a *ho'oponopono* session illustrates how dialogue in *ho'oponopono* can proceed and reveals the movement of various steps and phases of the process. It is a contemporary rather than traditional example, although it closely follows the outline just presented.

Ho'oponopono With a Hawaiian Family

This abbreviated example of a *ho'oponopono* session is based on a demonstration of the process that was videotaped for use by the Sub-Regional Child Welfare Training Center, School of Social Work, at the University of Hawaii.[14] The cast consists of family members who, for the the purpose of the demonstration, conceived and planned a contrived problem that they then acted out for the videotape. The *ho'oponopono* session that followed, however, was unrehearsed and seemed to tap genuine expressions of emotion. In the following account emphasis is given to dialogue examples and interaction patterns illustrating some of the more distinctive features of *ho'oponopono*. Other parts of the session are summarized.

The family chose the pseudonym "Kealoha." The family members include Mr. Kealoha; Mrs. Kealoha; Kalau and Kili, their two teenage daughters; Ka'ai'ai, their pre-teen daughter; and Kekumu, their young son.

Setting

The problem emerges on a Sunday morning during a debate among family members about whose turn it is to cook breakfast. Based on his understanding of an earlier agreement, Mr. Kealoha tells Kalau it is her turn to cook. Kalau becomes angry, since she cooked the day before. She says she will do it, but that it is unfair. Once in the kitchen, Kalau noisily bangs the dishes around and is visibly angry. When Kili and Mr. Kealoha come into the kitchen, Kalau speaks sharply to each of them and they in turn argue back. Later at the breakfast table with the whole family gathered, the tension mounts. Kili calls Kalau a "grump." Kalau scolds Kekumu for using his hands, rather than a spoon to eat. Ka'ai'ai and Kalau exchange sharp remarks and looks. Finally Mr. Kealoha intervenes, questioning what is happening. Frustrated, he suggests, "Well, it's about time we stop it for now and after breakfast we'll go *ho'oponopono*, O.K.?" The family members nod or grumble agreement and quietly finish breakfast.

The Ho'oponopono Session

The family gathers in the formal living room. Everyone is seated in a circle on the floor. Mr. Kealoha is the leader of the session. He first reminds them that they are there because of the things that happened that morning.

Mr. Kealoha: I think we need to resolve some of the differences that we have among ourselves. O.K.? Are you folks ready for this?

Others: Yeah.

They all join hands and bow their heads.

Mr. Kealoha: Let's join our hands and pray. Dear Heavenly Father, Creator of heaven and earth and to His only Son Jesu Cristo; Dear Lord, we thank thee for this opportunity to get together as an *'ohana,* a family. It was obvious during this morning that many things were happening to our family. People were getting at one another and things weren't right. As You know, we need to restore harmony within our family in order for us to continue on. Dear Lord, as we get together in this *ho'oponopono,* give us the strength and wisdom and understanding to be able to lay the problems out and identify what the problems are. Give us also the understanding and the know-how to be able to discuss things freely without hurting one another, and to say things in a way that makes for understanding. And, dear Lord, give us the opportunity, so that as one is talking about the problem, that the others will sit quietly and listen with an open ear, so that they can understand as to how the other one perceives what is happening. And, dear Lord, after we've identified it all, may we be able to open our hearts to one another, to forgive each other, so that we can then carry on. Always, we ask in Thy holy name. Amen.

The family members release their hands and raise their heads. Mr. Kealoha asks Mrs. Kealoha to begin with her side. She begins, "As I saw it this morning . . . ," and continues to describe her understanding of the cooking agreement. Originally, she says that she was pleased with the arrangement, but today she feels "disgusted" at Kalau's attitude and behavior. It further upsets her to see Kalau taking her anger out on her sisters and brother during breakfast.

Mr. Kealoha asks Mrs. Kealoha for clarification about the actual agreement by asking if each family member was present when it was made. She recalls that they were, although Kalau had gone in and out of the room during the discussions.

Mr. Kealoha then turns to Kili to discern her involvement. Kili admits that when she heard Mrs. Kealoha and Kalau arguing in the kitchen curiosity got the best of her and she entered the kitchen.

At this point Mrs. Kealoha begins to protest and Mr. Kealoha reminds her with gestures and words not to interrupt—that she has had her chance and that in *ho'oponopono* everyone has the chance to talk in peace while the others listen.

Kili admits that she had been *maha'oi* (bold, inquisitive) but says that Kalau did not have to shout at her. Mr. Kealoha asks her to explain more about the shouting episode; Kili does so. Mr. Kealoha then paraphrases and summarizes Kili's account.

Mr. Kealoha: So you recognize that the timing you went in was probably not correct?

Kili: Yeah.

Mr. Kealoha again paraphrases, this time recognizing that Kili's motives had been inquisitive but that she nevertheless did not like Kalau shouting at her.

Mr. Kealoha: What did you do after she shouted?

Kili: I snapped back at her.

Mr. Kealoha: But you did get back at her in a nasty way and created further *hihia* for the entanglement?

Kili: Yeah.

Mr. Kealoha then attempts to corroborate the account by asking Mrs. Kealoha, who had been present. Mrs. Kealoha says that she actually had asked Kili to come into the kitchen twice, once to set the table and later to ask her opinion about the terms of the cooking agreement. She also says that she recalls that Kili had seemed overeager to get involved.

Mr. Kealoha: *Maha'oi?*

Mrs. Kealoha: Yes.

Mr. Kealoha: Did Mommie state this correctly?

Kili: Yeah.

Kalau now has her opportunity to share. She describes the events of the morning and admits that she was upset at Mrs. Kealoha when Kili came into the kitchen. Kalau says that she "exploded" at Kili because she felt that Kili was defending Mrs. Kealoha.

Mr. Kealoha: You felt your sister was ganging up on you?

Kalau: Yeah.

Mr. Kealoha: So what did you say to her?

Kalau: "Get out of the kitchen!"

Mr. Kealoha: Is that normally the way you talk to each other?

Kalau: When I'm mad at her, yeah.

Mr. Kealoha: And then you argue back and forth?

Kalau: Yeah.

Mr. Kealoha: But that doesn't make for resolution. Am I correct?

Kalau: Yeah.

Mr. Kealoha then asks Kalau to explain more about what occurred at the breakfast table. Kalau complies, admits that she had snapped at the others "for revenge," then laughs.

Mr. Kealoha: Is that all? What about you and Mommie?

Kalau turns toward Mrs. Kealoha and gives her a dirty look and says, "Oh." Mr. Kealoha reminds Kalau to look at and speak to him. Kalau explains that she knew Mrs. Kealoha was disgusted with her, and she was angry in return. Mr. Kealoha asks Kalau to examine her actions at the time.

Mr. Kealoha: In *ho'oponopono*, we need to look at ourselves. Can you look at yourself and see how you contributed to the problem?

Kalau: Yeah.

The discussion goes on to reveal a basic misunderstanding about the cooking agreement. Kalau thought the agreement was that she was to cook one day out of the weekend. Since she had cooked the day before, she believed that she had fulfilled her responsibilities. Mr. Kealoha then asks Kalau if she had gone in and out of the room when the agreement was being made. She says that she had because she "didn't want to stay and listen." Mr. Kealoha admonishes Kalau that this behavior was not very wise since a decision had been made that affected her. He then paraphrases Kalau's story thus far and turns to Mrs. Kealoha for comments. Mrs. Kealoha begins but is interrupted when Mr. Kealoha speaks sharply to Kekumu, who has been slouching and not paying much attention to the discussion. He reminds Kekumu that they are working on a family problem and that Kekumu is a part of that problem and that he needs to be involved. Kekumu agrees and straightens up. Mrs. Kealoha defers discussing her side of the problems with Kalau because she thinks it is important to clear up the *hihia* between Kili and Kalau first.

Mr. Kealoha summarizes this *hihia,* as it was discussed earlier and proceeds.

Mr. Kealoha: Now are you folks ready to undo this with each other?

Kili and Kalau: Yeah.

Mr. Kealoha: Are you ready to *mihi?* Are you sure now?

They agree. He speaks to Kili.

Mr. Kealoha: Are you sure you understand what *mihi* is in terms of your interference with her?

Kili: Yeah.

Mr. Kealoha: O.K., can we start with Kili-Kili first? Kili, are you ready to *mihi?*

Kili: Yes.

At this point, Kalau and Kili face and speak directly to one another. Mrs. Kealoha is seated next to Kalau and pats her leg reassuringly during the *mihi.* Both girls are a bit teary as they speak.

Kili: Kalau, do you forgive me for putting my nose where it's not supposed to belong?

Kalau: Yes. Will you forgive me for snapping at you, because my anger was misplaced—it belonged to somebody else? And for giving you a double dosage at the table? (She wipes a tear from her cheek.)

Kili: Yeah. And me, for also barking at you—do you forgive me?

Kalau: Yeah. Do you forgive me too?

Kili: Yeah.

Both girls move across the circle toward one another and embrace. As they hug, they both cry and laugh a bit, then return to their places.

Mr. Kealoha turns to Kekumu next to clear up the difficulties between he and Kalau. Kekumu says has was angry at Kalau for snapping at him when he used his fingers instead of a spoon to eat, saying, "She uses her fingers sometimes too!" Mr. Kealoha interpreted that perhaps Kekumu objected not so much to what Kalau had said but to the way she said it. He also suggested that Kalau may have misdirected her anger. Mr. Kealoha asks Kalau for her side and she agrees that she did bark at Kekumu and recognizes that he didn't like it.

Mr. Kealoha: What are you going to do about it?

Kalau: Ask him for forgiveness.

Mr. Kealoha: Are you ready for that?

Kalau: Yeah.

Mr. Kealoha asks Kekumu if he is ready and he says he is. Kalau asks Kekumu for his forgiveness for her barking. Kekumu forgives her; they lean toward one another and hug.

A very similar discussion follows to unravel the *hihia* between Kalau and Ka'ai'ai. The problem was caused by Kalau misplacing her anger and speaking sharply to Ka'ai'ai. Since Ka'ai'ai responded in anger at the table, each had to ask the other for forgiveness.

The atmosphere in the session becomes quiet and serious, since it is now time to attend to the major problem between Mrs. Kealoha and Kalau. Mrs. Kealoha starts to speak, but then quietly begins to cry.

Mrs. Kealoha: Let me pull myself together.

Mr. Kealoha: Mommie needs to pull herself together because she feels—

Kekumu: Sad!

Mr. Kealoha: But also so that she can say things in a way that doesn't create more *pilikia* (trouble). O.K.?

Tissues are passed around to Kalau, Kili, and Mrs. Kealoha, and then Mrs. Kealoha begins to speak. She says that while listening today she realized that Kalau has a hard time talking to her. Also, in reflecting on past problems, she realizes that she often "digs in on" the kids when they do something wrong, and this treatment might be hard for Kalau to accept. She says that although Kalau had been going in and out of the room during the agreement, it was the parents' responsibility to make sure that the children clearly understood the agreement.

Mrs. Kealoha: And Kalau, I didn't check it out with you, and this *pilikia* might have been avoided. I have contributed by my failure—to not follow through to make sure that the communication was clearly understood.

Mr. Kealoha then paraphrases to Kalau two major points: Mrs. Kealoha gets after her when she thinks Kalau has done something wrong, and Mrs. Kealoha failed to check out the agreement because she assumed it was understood. Mr. Kealoha asks Kalau if she wants to share her thoughts.

Kalau: No, I think Mom said it all.

Mr. Kealoha: Well, what is this problem between you and Mommie?

Kalau explains that Mrs. Kealoha does not listen to her and that they argue back and forth. Mr. Kealoha suggests that perhaps when Kalau argues back Mrs. Kealoha also feels that Kalau has not heard what she had to say. Kalau agrees and Mr. Kealoha goes on to remind her about the importance of keeping "our big mouths shut" and listening to one another. He instructs her further:

Mr. Kealoha: After listening, and you still have a point to make, say it. But not in a hostile way, but in a way that makes for better understanding. Do you understand?

Kalau: Yeah.

Mr. Kealoha asks Mrs. Kealoha and Kalau if they are ready to *mihi*. They both nod and turn to one another. Mrs. Kealoha asks Kalau to forgive her for being angry, for snapping at her, and for not checking out the terms of the agreement with her. Kalau asks Mrs. Kealoha's forgiveness for banging around the kitchen and for taking her anger out on other family members.

Mr. Kealoha: Kalau, are you sure—once you forgive that it's *pau* (finished) already? Never a need to come up again?

Kalau: Yeah.

Mr. Kealoha turns to his wife.

Mr. Kealoha: Do you accept her forgiveness?

Mrs. Kealoha: Yes.

Kalau and Mrs. Kealoha embrace for a few moments. After they settle back into the circle Mr. Kealoha announces that he realizes that he needs to ask for forgiveness and asks if it is all right to turn over the *ho'oponopono* to Mrs. Kealoha. The family assents, and he admits fault for assuming that all the children understood the cooking agreement. He agrees that it is his responsibility as a parent to check things out. He also admits fault for getting angry at Kalau and for insisting that she cook, even though she had told him that she had already done her share. Kalau and Mr. Kealoha then *mihi* one another.

The family joins hands. Mrs. Kealoha summarizes some of the important lessons from the *ho'oponopono*. One lesson is that parents make mistakes and need to admit them, discuss them, and put them to rest. Mrs. Kealoha then asks forgiveness of each child in turn for assuming the agreement was understood. Mr. Kealoha repeats this *mihi* with each child also.

Mr. Kealoha asks if there are any further problems. Kalau makes an aside about a cramp in her leg from sitting so long. Everyone laughs, dispelling a lot of tension. Mr. Kealoha reminds the family that after *mihi* and *kala* there is *oki*. "Problems are laid to rest, not to be brought up again." He also reminds them that when they hurt one another, they hurt and disrupt the harmonious relationship with the "powers that be" and therefore they must ask forgiveness from them also.

Mr. Kealoha: Are you folks ready for that?

Family: Yes.

They bow their heads.

Mr. Kealoha: Dear Heavenly Father, Creator of heaven and earth, and to His only Son Jesu Cristo, we thank Thee for this opportunity in this *ho'oponopono,* to work out our family problems and difficulties; to identify the *hihia*—all the personal entanglements one with the other; to help us to discuss it in a way that does not create further hurts, but in a way that will lead to resolution of our problems. We also thank Thee for giving us the opportunity to listen so that we can understand how we ourselves have impacted on others, to examine ourselves, and in the communication one with the other, to be able to understand that possibly we may have contributed to the problems ourselves, whether by commission or whether by omission. And, dear Lord, we thank Thee for the opportunity for the *'ohana,* the family, to be here and to ask for forgiveness one from the other, to release and to let go, never more to come. And as we ask of you that as we hurt one another among ourselves, that we also hurt You, and we ask for Your forgiveness. Please forgive us. Please release and please set into the depths of the ocean our *pilikia,* never more to rise. All this we ask in Thy holy name. Amen.

The family members hug and kiss each other and rise.

SUMMARY

The Kealoha family's *ho'oponopono* illustrates how the components of the process fit together—how the process flows back and forth from leader to individual and leader to group and the spiritual deities. The prayers, discussions, and mutual forgiveness allowed the family to restore and strengthen their understanding of and caring for one another.

The session, albeit a contemporary example, had explicit Hawaiian threads: the occasional use of Hawaiian terms, the reinforcement of certain values such as strong family ties, the admonition against being *maha'oi,* the recognition that family troubles also disrupt spiritual harmony, and the use of metaphors, as exemplified in the closing prayer when Mr. Kealoha requested that the *pilikia* be "set into the depths of the ocean . . . never more to rise."

In chapter 3 most of the described uses of *ho'oponopono* depart more from the traditional form than the Kealoha example. But this example can be used as a point of reference to discern distinctions and consistencies among the other forms.

CHAPTER 1 NOTES

1. Concerning Mrs. Pukui, the authors stated: "Born in two cultures, she grew up knowing both. In her mother's family line were *kahunas*; in her father's background were the ways of New England. *Hānai*'d as an infant to her maternal grandparents, she was reared to be the family senior. This involved memorizing the old chants, rituals and customs, and learning the meanings and purposes of them. She spoke Hawaiian to her parents and grandparents; at school in Honolulu she was once punished for speaking her ancestral language; later with Dr. Samuel Elbert, she compiled five editions of the definitive *Hawaiian-English, English-Hawaiian Dictionaries*. Mrs. Pukui's childhood acquaintance with Hawaiian customs is reflected in her *Polynesian Family System in Ka'u*. Through the years she enlarged this knowledge by interviewing aged Hawaiians in other regions and other islands, by wide reading, and by translating the work of earlier Hawaiian historians. Today, at 77, she continues to travel and interview, recording her material for the Bishop Museum" (Pukui, Haertig, and Lee 1972, viii).

2. For further discussion of the issue of emics and etics in cross-cultural research, see Lonner (1979), Berry (1980), and Brislin (1981).

3. For more detailed information on traditional family life see *The Polynesian Family System of Ka'u, Hawaii* by Handy and Pukui (1972). A description of Hawaiian beliefs and practices more directly related to contemporary mental health and social welfare issues is found in *Nānā I Ke Kumu*, Volumes 1 and 2, by Pukui, Haertig, and Lee (1972) and Pukui, Haertig, Lee, and McDermott (1979). Other current resources are contained in McDermott, Tseng, and Maretzki (1980) and Kanahele (1982).

4. It is likely that *ho'oponopono* and other Hawaiian folk traditions have remained a family practice in some communities throughout the islands, even though they have lacked social visibility and prominence. As of this writing no survey or informal estimate of the prevalence of this type of use exists.

5. Taken from *The State of Hawaii Data Book, 1983*, Table 17, p. 40.

6. A few years ago I worked on a grant proposal that tried to resolve the dilemma of obtaining reliable ethnic categories. The principal investigator of the grant reported that there was little consensus among agencies in Honolulu about how to determine ethnicity. For example, the police department used verbal self-definition, and the Department of Education relied upon a 14-choice form to elicit "dominant ethnic background." Similar to American Indian and Native Alaskan groups, Native Hawaiians have debated defining group membership through a "blood quantum" determination.

7. Taken from *Native Hawaiian Study Commission Report*, Vol. I, 1983, Native Hawaiian Culture: Language, by Larry Kimura, p. 191.

8. Recently there has been a popular and humorous surge of interest in the use of pidgin, as evidenced by Simonson's fast-selling books *Pidgin to Da Max* (1981) and *Pidgin to Da Max Hanahou* (1982).

9. An overview of the salient points of Ito's study can be found in a 1982 article, "Illness as Retribution: A Cultural Form of Self-Analysis Among Urban Hawaiian Women," published in *Culture, Medicine and Psychiatry* 6:385–403.

10. See "Ho'oponopono: A Way to Set Things Right," *Honolulu Sunday Star-Bulletin and Advertiser,* July 18, 1971, p. B-8.

11. The questions raised in the project are some of the primary issues examined in this book. Paglinawan asked: "Can *ho'oponopono* be done by a non-Hawaiian? Is it transferable? Can it be used effectively in one-parent situations or in no-parent situations? Can it be used in community organization work with communities? Can it be used with non-Hawaiians?" (1972, 109–110). The answer to all these questions is yes, in that it has been used in all of these contexts. However, the question of measuring relative effectiveness in various settings remains an important issue for further study.

12. See Appendix A for a more complete description of *ho'oponopono* as it originally appeared in *Nānā I Ke Kumu* (1972).

13. Pukui et al. (1972, 74) report that retribution from the *'aumākua* would befall an individual who did not forgive when asked.

14. The title of the videotape is *"Ho'oponopono* With the Kealoha Family." An accompanying discussion guide has been written (Shook 1983).

CHAPTER 2

Culture, Change, and Mental Health Practices: Three Issues Related to Ho'oponopono Use Today

The primary purpose of this study is to provide descriptive material on innovative uses of an indigenous mental health practice. I believe that research allows room for the purely descriptive study—which has merit enough without extrapolating or reducing the information further.[1] However, my personal inclination is also to provide a basic theoretical context for this work, particularly since it is most certainly embedded and framed in the assumptions and questions posed by many other mental health researchers and practitioners. The increasing number of publications on the subject of culture and mental health is evidence of its burgeoning importance. Despite the relatively small size of the culture and mental health field, I believe that the premises and questions that have guided the field's research and practice provide valuable insights. One basic contribution comes from the use of a systems approach that recognizes and attempts to clarify the relationship and movement between what is pan-human, or universal, and what is group, or culture-specific and individually unique in each situation or interaction.

This chapter gives reference to some of the general works on culture, change, and mental health and explores three issues that have direct bearing on the contemporary uses of *ho'oponopono*. The first issue illustrates how the innovative use of *ho'oponopono* relates to a national human services trend that encourages the use of alternative means to meet the mental health needs of various minority groups. The second issue examines how the study of *ho'oponopono* may help discern which elements of therapy might be considered universal and which might be culture-specific. The last issue investigates some fundamental notions about the process of cultural change and provides a basis for understanding the different viewpoints expressed by individuals interviewed in this study, particularly regarding their thoughts on the uses of *ho'oponopono* in contemporary society. This chapter thus provides a broader context for readers who are interested in exploring the links to other research in the area of culture and mental health.

THE MOVE TOWARD CULTURALLY APPROPRIATE SERVICES

Social scientists, particularly anthropologists and psychologists, have been fascinated by the relationship of culture to the perception of self, the specific manifestations of disorders and their classification, and the various forms of psychotherapy and healing (Marsella 1982). Whereas much of the early research described beliefs and practices from so-called exotic cultural groups, today researchers attempt to formulate models and develop the beginnings of theories that will enable us to understand more clearly how culture affects perception and behavior. Marsella (1982) developed one model to illustrate the complex, dynamic factors at work in any behavior. A primary factor is the person who is affected by internal variables (both biological and psychological) and external variables (from both the cultural and physical environments). This person interacts in a particular situation, which produces a specific normal or abnormal behavior that has modifying effects on both the person and situation. Culture is both an explicit feature of this model, as part of the makeup of each person, and an implicit feature, as part of each situation and of the definition of what constitutes normal or abnormal behavior in a particular situation. Kleinman (1980) provides a theoretical framework for understanding the relationship of culture, illness, and psychiatry. His formulations, primarily based on empirical research conducted in Taiwan, stress the importance of understanding health care systems as they are embedded in the cultural context. Indeed, he suggests that the health care system is a cultural system. His is a holistic approach based on an examination of the various beliefs related to illness, the treatments that are prescribed for the illnesses, the roles and relationships among patients, healers and others, and the relationships among all these parts of the system.

If one truly recognizes and accepts the mediating cultural influence on the recognition and definition of psychological distress and on its manifestations, then it is obvious that treatments also must be cloaked in culturally suitable forms. For current mental health practitioners, the task begins with examining the assumptions that have pervaded modern approaches to treatment and ultimately involves developing modes of treatment that fit the variety of ethnocultural groups. In the United States, many mental health professionals recognize that minority ethnic groups have not received adequate or appropriate services, particularly in locales comprising a substantial nonwhite, non-middle-class population (Atkinson, Morten, and Sue 1979; Marsella 1980; Pedersen 1979; Sue and McKinney 1975; Sue and Sue 1977; Torrey 1972). Reports of the 1978 President's Commission on Mental Health Task Force bluntly name racism[2] as the most pervasive mental health problem today (volume 3, 786). The reports also suggest that many mental health programs have been responsible for latently underscoring racism by favoring methods and procedures suited for a largely white, middle-class clientele.

Marsella (1980), Pedersen (1979), and Torrey (1972) all point out that most mental health practices today are based on a medical model of health and illness derived from Western philosophical traditions that place a premium on rational, scientific thought. The alternative is to consider other methods, including those based on more unifying philosophies that do not separate physical, emotional, and spiritual factors in health and illness. These approaches may well be the predominant ones used in most cultures, except for those of, or strongly influenced by, the United States and Western Europe. Furthermore, Pedersen (1981) suggests that non-Western perceptions and values may be even better suited to ensuring a harmonious future in "Western" societies, since these societies will most likely be quite multicultural in makeup. Reynolds and Keifer (1977) also make a case for the benefits that Westerners might receive by participating in Asian strategies like Morita and Naikan therapy. The ideas of Pedersen and Reynolds and Kiefer directly relate to some of the issues surrounding *ho'oponopono* usage as described later in this book.

Another recommendation for creating a more balanced and comprehensive approach to mental health program development is to use existing natural helping systems that already may be functioning in the community (Frank 1971; Higginbotham 1976; Speck and Ruevini 1969; Sue 1978). Investigating the possibilities of incorporating indigenous or folk therapies into the treatment configuration has also been suggested (Draguns 1981a; Marsella 1980; Torrey 1972; Tseng and Hsu 1979). *Ho'oponopono* has been cited as an example of such an indigenous helping system by Draguns (1981a, 6), Pedersen (1979, 88), and Tseng and McDermott (1975, 382; 1981, 174).

Increasingly, authors are recommending ways to assess a cultural group's needs, definitions, communication styles, and expectations of mental health services (Atkinson, Morten, and Sue 1979; Higginbotham 1979; Ivey 1981; Sue 1981; Sundberg 1981). Models and practices derived from this kind of assessment theoretically would be more culturally sensitive than those not accounting for cultural variables. Draguns's advice to a prospective cross-cultural counselor shows the inherent complexity of this approach.

Be prepared to adapt your technique (e.g., general activity level, mode of verbal intervention, content of remarks, tone of voice) to the cultural background of the client; communicate acceptance of and respect for the client in terms that are intelligible and meaningful within his cultural frame of reference; and be open to the possibility of more direct intervention in the life of the client than the traditional ethos of the counseling profession would dictate or permit. (1981a, 11)

Conceivably, programs and methods that considered and utilized culturally relevant processes would be viewed as legitimate by the community since they reflected some of the values, beliefs, and practices of the group. This might, in turn, overcome one of the major concerns of the mental health profession—that many individuals do not utilize available mental health services because the services are perceived as being impotent or uncomprehending.

An increasing number of articles give suggestions for designing and implementing mental health programs suited for specific ethnic populations including native Americans (Edwards and Edwards 1980; Lewis and Ho 1979; Redhorse 1980; Richardson 1981; Trimble 1976; Youngman and Sadognei 1979), blacks (Bryson and Bardo 1979; Smith 1981), Asians (Brown, Stein, Huang, and Harris 1973; Kitano and Matsushima 1981; Sue 1981; Sue and Sue 1979), and Hispanics (Abad, Ramos, and Boyce 1974; Christiansen 1979; Delgado 1982; Gonzales 1976; Ruiz 1981; Ruiz and Padilla 1979).

Examples of Culture-based Mental Health Programs

Despite the recommendations for developing culturally appropriate services a lag exists in implementing such innovative approaches. The current literature, however, reveals some notable exceptions, some designed for specific ethnic populations while others have a multiethnic focus.[3] Geographically the programs are located in both urban and rural settings and span the United States and its territories. The following paragraphs summarize the types of service strategies used and highlight the details of a few programs.

A survey of approaches cited in eleven articles shows that integrated, multifaceted services are still the most popular. Conventional clinics using group and individual psychotherapy and/or chemotherapy are part of most programs. Some of these services are augmented by more innovative strategies, such as bilingual and paraprofessional staff and support networks. The literature also mentions, though less frequently, referrals to folk healers, maintenance of a resource center, provision for indigenous treatments, and use of community development and organization work.

A look at three of these programs, two for native American groups and one designed for a multiethnic community, will provide a better sense of how the approaches are combined to constitute a program.

The Papago Psychology Service was designed for a reservation-based tribe in Arizona (Kahn et al. 1975). The service employs a predominantly indigenous professional and paraprofessional staff and utilizes native healers when indicated as appropriate by the staff. Perhaps most significantly, policy and budgeting control is left in the hands of the tribe. Non-Papago psychologists, including those who had been instrumental in the project's design, are called in for consultation services only when the Papago staff members deem it necessary.

Another program for native Americans could be considered multiethnic since it serves urban natives in the San Francisco Bay area from more than a dozen tribal backgrounds (Fields 1979). Known as the Urban Indian Child Resource Center, the Oakland program contends with some of the problems associated with the federal government's controversial relocation program of the 1960s. An intertribal community and resource center is maintained, providing a gathering place for both educational activities and cultural celebrations. The center also has a comprehensive Indian child welfare program that includes an Indian Family Support Network to provide assistance when a native child needs foster care and the child's tribe or extended family is unable to help.

The Miami Community Mental Health Center model initially was designed to serve six ethnic populations by providing culturally appropriate treatments and by alleviating stresses in the environment that lessened the groups' abilities to use their adaptive resources (Lefley and Urrutia 1982). Mental health teams, based in neighborhood clinics, are the foundation of the program. The teams, of mostly indigenous mental health workers, are led by a social scientist and also include clinical, professional, and paraprofessional mental health workers. The leader acts as a "culture broker" (a term used by Weidman 1973) and is an important mediating link between the ethnic community and the formal medical system. Team services include chemotherapy, psychotherapy, neighborhood outreach, educational consultation, in-home and in-community direct services, ethnographic and demographic research, and community organization activities. This "Miami Model" of services is also one of the few examples of comprehensive cross-cultural training programs in the United States.

Relationship to Hoʻoponopono Use

The use of indigenous treatment approaches and indigenous healers is noted in some of the current literature. Fields (1979) reported the use of acupuncture as an adjunct treatment for Chinese clients with chronic insomnia, somatic complaints, or schizophrenia who had failed to respond to more conventional treatment methods. Use of traditional healers—the *suruhanos* on Guam (McMakin 1975), Puerto Rican spiritualists in New York (Garrison 1978), and the Papago tribal healers in Arizona (Kahn et al. 1975)—illustrates attempts by mental health professionals to integrate culture-specific methods with conventional treatment.

The contemporary uses of *ho'oponopono* described in this book are yet another example of this type of innovation. However, the case of *ho'oponopono* is different from most mental health innovations for two reasons. First, although it was traditionally used within the family setting, it has now been used in a wide variety of settings with unrelated people. Second, its use has extended beyond the Hawaiian community and is being led by and used with individuals from many other ethnic backgrounds. Some of the reasons for this divergence from traditional use patterns are given in the interviews, but a more thorough understanding of the implications of these changes will have to await further research.

THE SEARCH FOR THE EMIC-ETIC BALANCE IN THERAPY

A convincing case for using culturally appropriate and effective therapeutic methods was made earlier. However, discerning which elements of therapy have transferability across cultural lines and which are appropriate only within specific cultural boundaries is still an unfinished task. It is perhaps one of the most important and complex issues in cross-cultural mental health.[4] By examining the literature first on etics (universals) and then emics (cultural specifics) of therapy, we can begin to build a framework for understanding how *ho'oponopono* can be analyzed.

Therapeutic Universals

Jerome Frank has been influential in encouraging therapists and researchers to examine therapy in its historic and cross-cultural variability. His inquiries lead one to question what counts as psychotherapy.

> My own preoccupation has been an effort to isolate features of the psychotherapeutic relationship and the context of the therapeutic situation common to all forms of psychotherapy that may contribute to their success. Once the part played by these shared features has been identified, we may be better able to determine the differential effects of different techniques with different types of patients. (1971, 351)

Frank (1961) scrutinizes Western therapy, particularly psychoanalysis, religion and faith healing, and thought reform as types of healing systems having commonalities. After comparing these divergent forms, Frank concludes that three features are shared by all: (1) a trained, socially sanctioned healer, (2) a sufferer seeking relief, and (3) a series of contacts for the purpose of producing change. Later Frank (1971) updated and expanded this list to include six common factors: (1) strong, emotionally charged relationship, (2) a rationale or myth that explains the cause of the distress and gives possible techniques for its relief, (3) new information to aid the patient in understanding the problem and alternative ways of coping, (4) ways to strengthen the patient's expectations of help by mobilizing a sense of hope, (5) provision of an experience of success within or as a result of the therapy, and (6) "facilitation of emotional arousal."

Another pan-cultural view of therapy is presented by Torrey (1972). Torrey makes fun of what he calls the "psychiatric imperialism" of Western practitioners who seem to think that their etiology and prescriptive bag of tricks has a corner on the world therapeutic market. However, in his cross-cultural look at the mostly anecdotal accounts of therapist efficacy, Torrey concedes that psychiatrists are no more or less effective with Europeans and their descendants than are *curanderos* with Mexican-Americans in the barrio, *zars* with rural Ethiopians, or the shamans with the St. Lawrence Island Eskimos.

Like Frank, Torrey concludes that basic elements of therapy exist pan-culturally, although he categorizes these elements in a slightly different way. His first category is a shared world view between healer and client —something that makes possible what Torrey calls the "Rumpelstiltskin" principle. This metaphor alludes to the importance of the therapist's ability to name an illness correctly. Only when a state of "cognitive congruence" encompassing the meanings of language and nonverbal cues exists between healer and patient is an acceptable naming process possible. The second component is the need for a relationship. The therapist is seen as possessing special qualities that contribute to the relationship formation, although the exact nature of those qualities may be culturally relative.[5] The third factor involves the client's expectation of being helped, which is similar to Frank's mobilization of hope. Finally, the techniques used must fit within an accepted cultural framework.

In the above views therapy is primarily seen as an exogenous process, in that the relief of a person's suffering comes from interaction with an outside agent and is maintained by a special interpersonal relationship. This therapeutic interaction, which is fundamentally a communication process,[6] is carried out by a minimum of two individuals—the therapist (or healer, counselor, helper) and the client (or patient, sufferer). The client's problem or source of suffering is the focus of the interaction, and the therapist uses specific techniques to ameliorate the problem.

Another view of therapy concentrates more on the endogenous, or internal, healing mechanisms. These may be activated in the course of a therapeutic interaction or may be activated without the guidance or presence of a therapist. These endogenous phenomena are explored by Prince in a fascinating article. In it he takes issue with the narrow and conventional definitions of therapy. Prince states that the need for therapy arises from an individual's expression of his or her personal suffering. Psychotherapy is then seen as encompassing "any psychological procedure that is aimed at relieving an individual with such a complaint" (1980, 292). While not excluding more conventional "talk therapy" or other interactive procedures, Prince's definition legitimizes the benefits derived from sleep or isolation and altered states of consciousness like dreams, trance, mystic states, meditation, and shamanic ecstasy.

The Cultural Specifics of Therapy

Prince's perspective seems like a good place to shift the focus from etic to emic concerns, since many of the endogenous elements of therapy are more frequently included as legitimate from a within-culture viewpoint. The relationship between culture, illness, and therapy has been established by many authors cited earlier in this chapter. The interest in examining worldwide variations of therapy followed a number of anthropological and psychological studies in "culture-specific disorders."[7] Frank's and Torrey's works were influential, as well as was Kiev's (1964). More recently, the works of Lebra (1976), Kleinman (1980), and Marsella and White (1982) have expanded the references available.

The point reinforced by these authors is that therapy must be cloaked in the garments of the client's cultural milieu. Therapy is embedded in a cultural system that provides individuals with a way to understand their world, through a cosmological and normative framework. Some interesting work has been done to explain how specific therapies match the cultural system. Tseng and McDermott (1975) illustrate the relationship between Morita therapy in Japan and Zen Buddhist thought and practice. Murase (1982, 324) believes that certain Shinto religious traditions are even more fundamental in Morita and Naikan therapy than the obvious Zen Buddhist connections. In other examples, Torrey (1972) cites reasons why *curanderos* might be a preferred mental health resource for Mexican-Americans in certain California communities, while Frank (1961) links the popularity of psychoanalysis with Western European and American beliefs in rationality and science.

Another idea is that therapeutic systems reflect the cultural agenda by serving personal needs not met through normal daily routines. Therapy can be seen as compensating for the cultural system by providing a "time-out." Ritchie (1976) describes a widely used Maori version of time-out that allows an individual with a *Mate maori* (Maori illness as opposed to the kind amenable to Western therapeutic interventions) to declare himself or herself sick, go to bed, and receive help from relatives and friends. Ritchie enumerates the many positive therapeutic features of this respite and concludes that Western psychiatry would do well to examine and utilize the benefits of similar community-based healing opportunities. Tseng and McDermott (1975) point out that therapy itself can be a timeout, in that it allows individuals to behave in ways not permissible in other settings. Therefore, in societies that demand rigid and conforming behaviors, a cathartic healing system could provide an avenue for compensation and relief. The converse might hold true in more expressive or loosely knit societies.

Emics and Etics of Ho'oponopono

How then might *ho'oponopono* be examined as a therapeutic procedure with both universal and culturally specific features? Certainly it can be agreed that *ho'oponopono* is a therapeutic interaction, in that its purpose is to resolve a problem and ease the suffering within a family, with the assistance of a respected leader who uses specific rituals and techniques that are culturally sanctioned. The ingredients of primary sufferer, helper, problem, and method are all present in *ho'oponopono,* although because it is a group process recognizing that more than one person may "own" the problem, the so-called "client" role may shift during the sessions or may be held by more than one person at a time. In the Kealoha family's *ho'oponopono,* for example, all family members had an expressed part as both the injured and the injurer. Even the role of helper, or leader, had to shift when the father recognized his part in the problems. Although these dynamic qualities complicate the analysis of *ho'oponopono* as therapy, the essential elements are still evident.

In examining *ho'oponopono* using Frank's (1971) schema, it can be seen that it fits in the following ways:

1. It is used with people who have emotionally charged relationships with one another.

2. It has methods for uncovering and interpreting the cause of the problem (i.e., transgressions against another person or the *'aumakua* that disrupts the family's harmony) and the resolution (through honest and genuine discussion).

3. During the sessions individuals receive new information regarding the transgression (during the *mahiki* when those involved express their thoughts and feelings about the problem). Also during this phase suggestions may be given to participants on how to prevent reoccurrences, how to give and receive forgiveness, and how to make necessary restitution.

4. Entering into the sessions is cause for raised expectations of help, since, when entered into with good faith, the process usually continues until resolution occurs. In addition, since the family elders are respected, their leadership role gives hope and inspires greater attention to the process.

5. It provides a successful experience when the outcome of the sessions is problem resolution that restores harmonious family relationships.

6. Finally, it has emotional arousal mechanisms built into the procedures (through the *kūkulu kumuhana* and *pule,* which both focus on and strengthen the emotional commitment made to the participants and the process).

Ho'oponopono can also be validated using Torrey's classification of therapy:

1. Cognitive congruence among family members is likely to be quite high, which makes possible a correct naming of the causes of the problem and the course of the treatment in terms understood by the participants.

2. The relationship qualities of the process are enhanced through the role of the respected and trusted leader.

3. There are expectations of being helped, particularly because of the perceived grave consequences of not resolving the difficulties.

4. The techniques used certainly fit within the Hawaiian cultural framework and are accorded prestige and respect.

Although the *ho'oponopono* system appears to be primarily an exogenous process that heals family relationships through interaction, an endogenous component may exist as well. In one of the examples of *ho'oponopono* sessions given in *Nānā I Ke Kumu* (Pukui, Haertig, and Lee 1972, 64–67), a client shared the contents of a dream that had considerable bearing on insights into the nature of the problem being discussed. Dreams, visions, portentous symbols, and precognitive messages (extrasensory perception) are experienced by many Hawaiians and accorded prominent value in providing interpretations of past events and for giving guidance regarding future actions.[8]

Ho'oponopono is obviously a culture-specific process. The terms used are part of the Hawaiian language and derive from Hawaiian beliefs and customs. *Ho'oponopono* differs from most Western therapeutic practices in at least three other ways—the spiritual focus, the articulation of forgiveness and release, and the ritualized, built-in system of controls and steps.

Spiritual values have been an important part of Hawaiian life, and the use of *kūkulu kumuhana* and *pule* bolsters the family or group member's efforts by enlisting spiritual guidance and reinforcing the individual's relationship with each other and their God or gods. As demonstrated in the Kealoha family example, after the family members had cleared up the problems with one another, they needed to ask forgiveness from "the powers that be"; this indicates an understanding that spiritual forces are an integral part of family life.

The practice of articulating mutual forgiveness and release is the second distinguishing feature of *ho'oponopono*. In many therapies forgiveness may be implied, but it is rarely made an explicit part of the process. In *ho'oponopono,* however, it is mutual forgiveness that paves the way for individuals to let go of the problem and restore harmonious relations with other family members. Mutual forgiveness was traditionally so important that failure to forgive was among the most serious offenses a person could commit. Unrelenting grudge holding was not only cause for being cut off from the family, but it threatened an individual's relationship with the spiritual forces in ways that could jeopardize the spiritual, physical, and emotional well-being of the individual or innocent family members.

Finally, *ho'oponopono* is a ritualized and highly structured process that has built-in controls and steps that are to be followed. An example of one control is the insistence that the disagreeing family members refrain from directly addressing one another during the discussion phase. Another example is the guideline that discourages participants from acting out their intense feelings and urges them instead to talk about their views in as calm a manner as possible. This is seen as a way to keep the problem from escalating further. Another control feature is *ho'omalu,* the cooling-off period of silence and reflection that is used to interrupt angry or other disruptive behaviors. These control mechanisms may be examples of suppressive therapeutic strategies designed to provide a balance in a culture that generally encourages expressions of emotion and gregariousness.

In summary, it appears that *ho'oponopono* does indeed have universal elements of therapy that are presented in ways that arise from and complement Hawaiian social structure, beliefs, and practices. The culturally relevant features give *ho'oponopono* the legitimization needed for effective therapy to occur with people of Hawaiian ancestry. But what can we say about some of the uses of *ho'oponopono* that are presented later in the case studies that do not fall within the traditional framework? As noted earlier, the case materials show that *ho'oponopono* has now been used in a wide variety of settings with people who were not part of an *'ohana* and not part of the Hawaiian ethnic community. What is it about this process that transcends cultural boundaries? I believe that a thorough response to this question is beyond what we now know about culture, therapy, and *ho'oponopono,* but the individuals who share their experiences through the case studies will take us a small step closer to understanding what makes a successful therapy-client match.

INDIVIDUAL RESPONSES TO CULTURAL CHANGE

This last issue is an investigation of some questions about the process of cultural change itself. Although diverging somewhat from the more clinical emphases of the previous two issues, it reflects a dilemma I faced quite early in the research process. The situation concerned individual reactions to the original premise of the study—examining "adaptations" of *ho'oponopono.* One person declined to be interviewed on his use of the process because of his objection to the use of the word "adaptation." He believed that any departure from the form and context of *ho'oponopono* as explained by Pukui was probably not really *ho'oponopono* and should be called something else. Concern about preserving the process's integrity was shared by almost all participants in the study, although definitions of what constituted "integrity" in this case varied. I labeled this the "form versus essence" dilemma. It prompted me to look at the assumptions underlying the study and to investigate more deeply the nature of culture and cultural change in order to find out if it is possible to determine the degrees of authenticity of a cultural practice. For example, to investigate the authenticity of *ho'oponopono* as a cultural practice, one might ask, "When do changes in *ho'oponopono* become significant enough to produce a qualitatively different practice?"

My inquiry led me to learn more about attitudes toward cultural change, particularly when the change is part of a revitalization movement. Examining attitudes about change is especially pertinent to this study because the popularity of *ho'oponopono* coincides with a general movement in Hawaii to unearth, affirm, and sustain Hawaiian cultural values, beliefs, and practices. Kanahele (1982) has identified this movement as a period of Hawaiian renaissance. Issues related to cultural change are complex, have enormous implications, and are rooted in some of the major theoretical queries in social science. As such, doing justice to the issues is beyond the scope of this work. Yet because the questions about some of the issues have permeated the research, albeit implicitly in most cases, it is worthwhile to point out how they are related to the work presented here.

First, this study assumes that culture is a dynamic, complex, and constantly changing process. Tylor (1874, 1) gave a classic definition of culture: ". . . a complex whole which includes knowledge, belief, art, morals, law, custom and other capabilities and habits acquired by man as a member of society." In 1952 Kroeber and Kluckholn articulated a defi-

nition of culture that was based on an analysis of several hundred definitions of culture (Kluckholn 1962, 181).

> Culture consists of patterns, explicit and implicit of and for behavior
> acquired and transmitted by symbols, constituting the distinctive achieve-
> ment of human groups, including their embodiments in artifacts; the essen-
> tial core of culture consists of traditional (i.e., historically derived and
> selected) ideas and especially their attached values; culture systems may, on
> the one hand, be considered as products of action, on the other as condi-
> tioning influences upon further action.

In both these definitions, change is implicit as the mode of transmitting
culture. Neither definition explicitly uses the word "change" as a feature,
which perhaps reflects the perception held by some people (not social scientists, for whom the understanding of the reality of change is assumed)
that culture is a static collection of things and ideas. Geertz (1973, 144)
shows how functional theories of culture have failed to adequately
describe and incorporate the dynamic changes of social organizations.
The bias of the functional approach is that changes in ritual patterns are
ones of progressive disintegration that destabilize the culture. Perhaps
this was also the bias of the man who refused to participate in the study
—the acceptance of the premise that ho'oponopono might have a range
of applications and forms that could be seen as furthering the disintegration of Hawaiian culture.

Barnett (1953) contributed enormously to the understanding of cultural change in his work, *Innovation: The Basis of Cultural Change*. His
definition of an innovation is "any thought, behavior or thing that is new
because it is qualitatively different from existing forms" (p. 7). Does the
current use of ho'oponopono qualify as an innovation in this sense? We
must look more closely at Barnett's work to understand why it does.

> In one respect, old ideas that are revived or borrowed to meet a crisis must
> be classified as innovations. If they have been *borrowed or taken out of
> other contexts of time*[9] and place, they must almost inevitably be modified
> to conform to existing modes and requirements. (1953, 81)

Indeed, the emergence of ho'oponopono as a tool that could be
employed in a professional social work setting came about because of the
young social worker's crisis—his failure to understand the nature of the
troubled Hawaiian boy's problem, which led him to use approaches that
could assist the family through their troubles. Furthermore, all examples
of ho'oponopono used in this study have been adapted at least to a new
setting and in many cases have also been used for audiences not originally
envisioned.

Although innovations sometimes seem to appear out of nowhere, they of course do not. Innovations are described as mental patterns that are created when two or more preexisting cognitive configurations are recombined. The recombination processes take place in the mind of an individual and are constrained by the cultural, biological, psychological, social, and environmental experiences of that person (Barnett 1953). To illustrate this in a general way, it can be said that each of the individuals in this study who decided to use ho'oponopono had in his or her mind a model or prototype of a group problem-solving pattern or a helping interaction pattern. This familiar configuration may have helped them recognize ho'oponopono as a similar strategy that they could use in their work with groups.

The propensity of individuals to initiate creative and innovative solutions to problems appears to be inherent in human nature. However, according to Wallace (1970), it is not as common for individuals to accept innovations when they are on the "receiving end." He reports that a number of variables affect whether or not innovations are adopted. The variables include the nature of the innovation, the attributes of the individual or group advocating the change, and the personality and experiences of the individual contemplating the change. The study here presents some individual attitudes toward various uses, both actual and potential, of ho'oponopono. Although there may be insufficient evidence in each case study to fully understand the attitudes, the reader should keep in mind that the attitudes are based on a very complex interaction of variables.

One of the variables that is more open for examination is the degree to which the recent popularization of ho'oponopono is linked in people's minds with a more general renaissance of Hawaiian cultural beliefs and practices. In fact, two of the individuals interviewed believe that the work done in reviving ho'oponopono may have been one of the initial sparks in the renaissance movement. The history of the United States and the developing nations of the world in the 1960s and 1970s documents major changes in the role of minority groups in society. The term "minority groups" can refer to ethnicity—for example, any nonwhite group. It can also refer in a broader sense to factors such as powerlessness (i.e., women, the poor) or to "not the norm" (i.e., tall, short, fat, skinny, old, young, meditator, Catholic, homosexual, and so on). Shifts in minority group roles can be viewed as one kind of revitalization movement that can be outlined in stages. Initially, the group is rooted in a steady state period where there is acceptance of the status quo. Emergence of increased periods of dissonance and dissatisfaction leads to the rejection of dominant group patterns and the embracing of minority patterns—for example, in ethnic groups, a reawakening to the indigenous culture. Acceptance of a new reorganized steady state caps the process.[10]

A number of authors have characterized this process in slightly different ways. In more political terms, Bulhan (1980, 105–106) articulates a theory of what he terms "cultural in-betweenity." He names three stages that reflect the reactions of a group to domination by others: (1) capitulation (to the new culture); (2) revitalization (of the indigenous culture); and (3) radicalization (a new synthesis of both cultures). In the mental health field Atkinson, Morten, and Sue (1979, 194–197) outline an identity development model that not only lists the stages but also gives information about attitudes that often accompany these stages and makes recommendations about working with individuals in the various stages. The authors' Minority Identity Development Model has five stages: (1) conformity (characterized by a preference for the dominant culture); (2) dissonance (when confusion and conflict reign); (3) resistance and immersion (rejection of the dominant culture and complete affirmation of the minority culture view); (4) introspection (the search for individual autonomy and discomfort with complete adherence to the minority stance); and (5) synergetic articulation and awareness (an integration of personal and cultural identity allowing for individual flexibility and also rejection of any form of oppression of one group by another).

The various reactions to the idea of adapting ho'oponopono may be related to the attitudes toward the Hawaiian renaissance movement. Both Hawaiians and non-Hawaiians may perceive the consequences of "adapting" a Hawaiian practice as being an almost irreligious act that damages the integrity of values and tradition. Others may perceive its contemporary use as a way to strengthen and reinforce the presence of Hawaiian practices in modern life. Still others may see the decision to use or not use ho'oponopono as a pragmatic issue related to discerning what "works" as a problem-solving method regardless of the specific cultural attributions or implications.

Once again, more questions are raised than the study can adequately consider, but these are issues that both subtly pervade the research and stand as a structural girder for the research details that follow.

SUMMARY

Chapter 2 puts the specific Hawaiian practice of ho'oponopono into a broader context, linking it to ideas about culture, change, and mental health practices. First the trend toward providing culturally appropriate treatment methods is examined. The contemporary uses of ho'oponopono are seen as part of this trend, inasmuch as ho'oponopono is an

indigenous method and a natural helping system of Hawaiians. However, because its use has extended beyond the traditional purposes and
audiences, ho'oponopono differs from most of the examples of innovative culture-based services cited in the literature today.

Discerning the universal and culture-specific elements of therapeutic
systems is listed as another major task in the mental health field. Some
basic schemas of emic and etic components of therapy are presented, and
ho'oponopono is examined in light of these schemas. The conclusion formulated is that ho'oponopono does indeed have the necessary elements
of therapy, in the broadest sense of the term, and has a number of features that derive from and address the specific Hawaiian cultural configuration. Again, ho'oponopono is found to be unusual compared with
most other non-Western therapies since it is being used by both Hawaiians and non-Hawaiians. Of course Western psychotherapy has been,
and is being, used cross-culturally (and has been both supported and
severely criticized for this), but aside from limited recent use of Morita
and Naikan therapy in the West (Reynolds and Keifer 1977), there are
few other occurrences of deliberate cross-cultural adaptations of non-
Western therapies to Western groups.

Finally, because I received such a wide range of comments on the relative merits or problems associated with the very notion of utilizing
ho'oponopono outside the traditional context, I present my understanding of the relationship of these attitudes to the process of cultural change.
Only rudimentary notions about this relationship could be discerned and
much remains to be considered. It may be that attitudes toward the use of
ho'oponopono today are related to an individual's attitudes about the
Hawaiian renaissance movement of the last fifteen years or are related to
a pragmatic cultural view of group problem-solving methods.

Since the contextual setting has been provided—the Hawaiian cultural
matrix presented in chapter 1 and the social science links in chapter 2—it
is time to let the stories of ho'oponopono be told.

CHAPTER 2 NOTES

1. See Cottle (1977) for more discussion on this research perspective.

2. I recognize that the term "racism" has become overused and therefore wide-
ranging in connotation. In this usage I believe that it most closely approximates
the definition: the belief or practice that one or more groups of people are supe-
rior to other groups, with physical characteristics being the primary determinant
of differentiation. A milder meaning of the term would include discriminatory
attitudes and treatment given by some groups to others due to ignorance or insen-
sitivity. The differences targeted in this case might include cultural beliefs, values,
and practices as well as physical characteristics.

3. One omission in this survey is blacks. Little information was found in the

literature on programs specifically designed for blacks. I could not find enough evidence to speculate on the reasons for this.

4. Draguns (1975, 1981a, and 1981b) repeatedly listed the emic-etic dilemma as a key issue in cross-cultural mental health.

5. For example, in the United States where individual autonomy and openness are valued, therapist qualities of genuineness, warmth, and empathy are found to be significantly related to effective psychotherapy (Truax and Carkuff 1967). However, in other ethnocultural settings, including minority groups within the United States, these may not be the critical traits, or at least the traits may be defined or demonstrated differently.

6. For further amplification of the relationship of communication to therapy, see Reusch and Bateson (1951); Reusch (1967); Ivey and Authier (1971); Scheflen (1973); and Bandler and Grinder (1976).

7. Marsella (1982) gives a historical overview of these shifts in research interests in cross-cultural mental health.

8. Once again *Nānā I Ke Kumu* is a treasure-hold of information on these phenomena. In particular, volume 2, chapters 4 (Dreams and Symbols) and 7 (Extrasensory Perception, Prophecies and Close Observations), are rich and rewarding reading.

MacDonald and Oden (1977) also provide further evidence of the validity of these internal mechanisms for problem solving among Hawaiians. They cite three case histories of adolescents experiencing hallucinations who had not responded to conventional treatment using desensitization techniques. The youths responded favorably when guided in a more culturally meaningful way to face the visions and the messages contained in them.

9. Author's emphasis.

10. For further investigation of this topic, see Adler (1974).

CHAPTER 3

The Case Studies

In this chapter the various uses of *ho'oponopono* take form as the eight individual case studies are presented. Before undertaking this research I had not been very concerned with the nitty-gritty details of how a researcher actually conducted interviews and made observations. I accepted and appreciated reading case studies or descriptive materials without knowing about the time-consuming and tedious tasks involved in gathering information and transforming raw interviews and field notes into a final presentation. When I began my own research and needed to learn some of these tasks I discovered that ethnographic reports, case studies, and other qualitative research papers often were vague about how research material findings came to life. Not only did this make it difficult for me to learn about various methodological styles, but it also made it difficult to assess the reliability of the reports. Therefore, the case studies in this work are prefaced by a description of the methods I used for selecting and interviewing *ho'oponopono* leaders and for reviewing, analyzing, and presenting the salient features of the study.[1] This methodological outline is followed by relevant characteristics of the individuals as a group. Finally, within a standardized framework, descriptions of eight individual uses of *ho'oponopono* are given.

HOW THE INTERVIEWS WERE CONDUCTED

All the individuals considered for participation in this study had recent experience leading *ho'oponopono* sessions as a part of their employment. Eight individuals who were asked to participate consented; one person declined.[2]

A moderately structured, open-ended interview was the main source of gathering information from the individuals.[3] The following paragraphs describe the measures taken to prepare for and conduct the interviews and later to analyze the materials gained from them.

An interview guide was designed before contact was made with the individuals for the interview. The guide's major purpose was to prepare the interviewer by providing a checklist of major topics to be covered in the interview. Two Hawaiians, who are recognized in their jobs as experts on Hawaiian mental health concepts including *ho'oponopono,* assisted in writing the guide. With their help important topical components, especially those most likely to be hidden from the scrutiny of a non-Hawaiian, were included.[4] (A copy of the guide is found in Appendix 2.)

The next step was to contact individual *ho'oponopono* leaders to see if they would consent to be interviewed for the study. I began with five names and also was referred to two agencies reported to be using the process. From these referrals I contacted three additional people who completed the sample.[5]

At least one preliminary meeting was arranged with each person to explain the purpose of the study, to outline the interview procedure, and to set up an appointment for the interview. This preliminary meeting took place with all but one individual who, because of an extremely busy schedule, could fit in only one meeting. The first part of his interview was spent reviewing the preliminary information.

The interviews occurred in a variety of settings, most commonly at the individual's place of work. One interview took place at my place of work and another was conducted in an individual's home. Generally two hours were set aside for the interviews, but they actually ranged from 1.5 to 3.5 hours.

Each interview was tape-recorded. In seven cases the individual first responded to open-ended queries about his or her experiences using *ho'oponopono* (i.e., "What does it mean? How did you come to use it? What other comments do you have about its use?"). One individual felt that the open-ended segment was too unstructured and requested that the interview guide be used as the format for the entire interview. After the open-ended part of the interview, I followed with questions from the interview guide. In the instances when a question on the guide had been covered earlier, the response to the question was restated in summary, as a means to provide for further reflection. This gave the individual an opportunity to elaborate on the subject if inclined to do so. Raising questions from the guide that had not been covered in the open-ended interview segment gave the individuals a chance to examine their experience of *ho'oponopono* in a new light. Since most of the topics in the guide were in rough form, the individual responses were invaluable in helping me to clarify and specify more useful and articulate ways of asking questions. The guide was thus used as a flexible tool that gave me clues for discovering what the salient features of analysis would be. After each interview the tapes were reviewed and extensive notes, including much verbatim material, were taken.

Additional notes were kept on my contact with participants before, during, and after the interviews. These notes were recorded in a field notebook. Reconstructions of conversations, methodological observations, analytical notes, and personal reactions to the interviews were included in this record. I was also a participant observer in one program where two of the leaders used ho'oponopono and recorded notes on this experience.

Combined, the interview notes and the field notes made up a set of working notes that were coded and analyzed. The categories of analysis were suggested from three sources. The first source was a set of questions that I had formulated when I began the research: (1) What were the reasons that led the individual to use ho'oponopono? (2) How did the individual learn to use the practice? (3) Were guidelines used to determine how and under what circumstances ho'oponopono would be used? If so, what were they? (4) What were the perceived changes that occurred in ho'oponopono as a result of its use in a nontraditional setting? (5) What is the individual's evaluation of the efficacy of ho'oponopono? (6) What difficulties were encountered while using the practice? (7) What are the recommendations to others who might want to use it?

Another source of specific categories came from the interview guide topics. Specific details on the style and procedures of ho'oponopono emerged here. Finally, during the process of reviewing the working notes, new empirical categories surfaced.[6] Chapter 4's ho'oponopono model was constructed from the working notes of two interviews and from additional conferences with one of the leaders. These conferences, which were not taped, were designed to check the reliability of the information in the notes and analysis and allowed the individual to elaborate on particular details of a complete ho'oponopono format that might be useful for future practitioners.

OVERVIEW OF THE CASE STUDIES

Who are the people who have used ho'oponopono, and what are their similarities and differences when viewed as a group? Four men and four women ranging from age 28 to "between 60 and 65" made up the sample. Three of them listed their ethnicity as Hawaiian or part-Hawaiian; four as Caucasian and one as Filipino. With only this information, the group seems quite heterogenous. However, as the interviews proceeded, some similarities in training and education became apparent.

Seven of the eight individuals had previous training or education in what I have categorized as "human relations." This label includes experiences in counseling, interpersonal communication, group process, humanistic education, Gestalt therapy, encounter group, parent effectiveness, social work, or other clinical programs. The eighth person was not formally trained but had been hired as a paraprofessional counselor because of his personal qualities and skills. This commonality may be indicative of a number of things. Possibly it shows that individuals with this type of background are attracted to ho'oponopono; perhaps they find an affinity with it based on underlying values and processes in human relations that are similar to ho'oponopono. It may also indicate that some background in human relations training is a prerequisite for attempting to use this complex process in a contemporary setting. Some of the individuals thought this was true.

The seven who had prior human relations experience also had at least a bachelor's degree. Five had master's degrees and one had a doctoral degree. The paraprofessional mentioned before had some college experience but less than a bachelor's degree level. The tendency toward advanced educational degrees may also have some bearing on the decision to use ho'oponopono.[7]

Other dimensions reveal similarities and differences that may have implications for the information given during the interviews; these include the way the individuals learned about ho'oponopono, the length of time they had used it, and the range of settings in which they had used it. The three part-Hawaiian individuals learned about ho'oponopono directly from Mary Kawena Pukui, as participants in the QLCC Culture Committee discussions. All of the others learned indirectly from Pukui through reading Nānā I Ke Kumu (1972). In addition, a few individuals had attended lectures on ho'oponopono but insisted that Nānā I Ke Kumu remained their primary resource.

Not surprisingly, the three part-Hawaiians who were on the Culture Committee had used parts of ho'oponopono or the complete process over the longest period of time; one individual had used the process since 1963. Two of the three also had the most extensive experience using the process in various settings, from working with Hawaiian families to working with unrelated non-Hawaiian groups.[8] The other five individuals had used ho'oponopono primarily within the context of their jobs. Three of the five used ho'oponopono for several years during a summer outdoor educational program; the other two used it for more than two years on a daily basis with young men in a drug abuse treatment program.

A final component that warrants examination concerns the relationship of each individual with the interviewer. I had considerably different relationships with each of them. I had worked closely with three participants for up to two years. I had met and spoken with two others about the project a few times before its inception. I met the other three shortly before the interviews specifically to request their participation in the project. These varied relationships may have a bearing on the following issues: (1) the amount of information shared during the interview, (2) the degree to which I understood the information shared, and (3) the quality of the information given, particularly the degree to which problems and concerns about ho'oponopono were shared. Although I think it merits stating the issues, I am not prepared to draw conclusions about a direct link between my relationships with the individuals and the results of the interviews. One way I adjusted for the variation was by taking more time with individuals I did not know to establish comfortable relationships with them. I accomplished this via telephone conversations and the preliminary meetings. I also checked the reliability of information provided by cross-checking with the individuals who had worked with each other or who had used ho'oponopono in the same program or setting. All participants were given the opportunity to review their case studies to check for accuracy and interpretation of the findings.

Each of the individuals has been given a pseudonym. The names of the agencies and programs have also been omitted. This measure of confidentiality was taken not so much to protect those interviewed, but to protect clients and others who participated in the ho'oponopono sessions who had no way of knowing that those sessions would later receive public attention.[9]

Table 1 lists the names given to the participants and provides a summary of some of the general characteristics discussed earlier. Prior training in human relations is noted. Highest educational degree earned, ethnicity, and sex are given. Also listed is the breadth of experience; this factor is ordered as high, medium, or low depending upon the amount of experience in using ho'oponopono and the number of various contexts in which the leaders have used the process. The relationship with the interviewer is also ordered as high involvement, medium involvement, or low involvement, coinciding with the amount of contact between each individual and the interviewer prior to the interview.

Keeping these factors in mind while reading the case studies may shed additional light on understanding variations in the individual's ability to articulate the process, share his or her ideas about its value, and make recommendations for others who might contemplate using ho'oponopono in the future.

Table 1
General Characteristics of Leaders

Name	Sex	Ethnic Background	Age	Prior Training in Human Relations	Highest Education Degree	Breadth of Experience Using Ho'oponopono	Relationship with Interviewer
Virginia Wahler	F	Caucasian	55	X	MA	Medium	High involvement
Robert Padua	M	Filipino	34		HS diploma	Low	Medium involvement
Jean Baker	F	Caucasian	30	X	MS	Medium	Low involvement
Joseph Whitney	M	Caucasian	28	X	BA	Medium	Low involvement
Paul Ellis	M	Caucasian	36	X	Ph.D.	Low	Low involvement
Keola Espiritu	M	Hawaiian	44	X	MSW	High	Medium involvement
Kalau Souza	F	Hawaiian	early 60s	X	MSW	Low	Medium involvement
Lani Espiritu	F	Hawaiian	42	X	MSW	High	High involvement

EIGHT CASES OF HO'OPONOPONO USE

Each of the eight leaders is considered individually in this section. The first part of each case study explores the context of use and begins with personal information on the person interviewed. Also included is information on the setting and on the audience with which *ho'oponopono* was used. In some examples, the use of *ho'oponopono* was a regular part of a program; if so, the program is described so it is possible to see how *ho'oponopono* fit with other program features.

The second part of each case study concentrates on comments that reflect each individual's attitudes about *ho'oponopono*. The topics covered refer to six areas of questioning.

1. How did the individual learn about *ho'oponopono?*
2. What does the person believe is the purpose of the practice?
3. What is his or her personal assessment of its impact?
4. What adaptations of the process have been made, and what are the individual's attitudes about its use?
5. What problems or barriers were encountered using the process?
6. While using *ho'oponopono,* what issues arose that might lead to useful recommendations for others considering using the process?

Quoted material used in this section is taken from notes of the taped interviews. The leader's own words are used without converting local idioms to standard English. Oral language has a richness and rhythm that is distinct from written communication. The reader who is able to "listen" to, rather than just read, the written forms may gain a better understanding of the different experiences of *ho'oponopono*.

All interviews took place between January and March 1981.

Virginia Wahler

Context of Use. Virginia has resided in Hawaii since 1973. She is an extremely warm and energetic woman who has a background in education and additional training in counseling—primarily transactional analysis—and communication/human relations. Creativity and communication are two long-standing personal interests that she weaves into whatever she does. Virginia lists "spiritual development" as a primary personal goal during recent years.

In her work in Hawaii she has concentrated on designing and implementing programs for young people who are in danger of becoming seriously delinquent and alienated. In 1979 she had the opportunity to bring her dream—a program for a "positive youth development model" —to fruition. Funded by a national drug abuse agency, this program was designed as a three-year action-research project with two primary goals: to study the effects of multiple drug abuse on male adolescents and to explore the effects of an innovative residential treatment approach that utilized a camp setting, emphasized education, environment, and culture, and enhanced self-concept through positive interaction and successful experiences.

The program brought four groups of about fifteen boys each to a residential camp setting for a six-month period of treatment. The in-residence period was followed by a five-month in-community follow-up period and another five-month period in the community without supervision. A variety of test measures were given at the inception and completion of each phase. The results were compared with those from selected control groups.

In managing the program, Virginia was guided by two questions she taught the boys to ask when making decisions: "Will it work?" (i.e., achieve the desired result), and "Does it honor everyone involved?" Virginia stated that the role of *ho'oponopono* in the program was as "a primary spiritual element, as well as our major therapeutic counseling tool." It was also a vehicle for emphasizing Hawaiian cultural traditions, a major value in the program since many of the boys were part-Hawaiian. Virginia used it with both the boys and the camp staff.

Comments About Ho'oponopono. Virginia knew a little about *ho'oponopono,* but it really made an impact upon her when she heard a presentation on the process by Keola Espiritu, another individual in the case study. At this point, Virginia reported, she began "to explore *ho'oponopono* for me—for how I could use it." Later, while she was writing the drug abuse project proposal, she read volume 1 of *Nānā I Ke Kumu* and learned more specifically about *ho'oponopono.* "As I see it, *Nānā I Ke Kumu* defined it as it was originally, as it is intended to be, and how it works."

And she believes the purpose stated in the book is best:

Setting things to right—because we teach so much about balance or harmony. Our body, mind, emotions, and spirit need to be in balance. That's what I call being "together." And they (the boys) are not "together" when they come to us—inside themselves. So we work on all four sides of man. And *ho'oponopono* is a process for putting things to right, back in balance, within the individual, and within their *'ohana.*

Ho'oponopono was used to solve problems that came up in the group as well as to reaffirm positive individual and group behavior. Because it was used on a daily basis, it helped cement the relations of the group and became a prevention tool. It was also a time during the day that the boys could share things like: "I had a good day. . . ." "I like this. . . ." "We had good fun doing this. . . ." "Things going good. . . ." "No problem. . . ." and "We had a problem, but we settled it before we got here."

After using the process every day for a few months the boys began to use *ho'oponopono* informally among themselves during the day to resolve minor problems that arose. Unfortunately, after the boys left the six-month residential portion of the project and returned to the community, they had few opportunities to continue using *ho'oponopono*. Follow-up care, which was provided for five months in the community, included *ho'oponopono* sessions with some but not all the groups. Virginia was disappointed that it was not as strong a feature of after-care as she had hoped. Program evaluations indicated that few boys took their experiences of using *ho'oponopono* back to their families. A notable exception was one Hawaiian boy who had shared the practice with his family and taught it to his friends.

According to Virginia's evaluation of the project, about 85 percent of approximately 50 boys who resided at the camp at the time of the interview have done very well upon returning to the community. She believes that *ho'oponopono* was one of the main causes of the success. Toward the end of our interview she laughed and said, "I would hate to think of trying to do this program—even with everything else—but without *ho'oponopono!*"

Virginia realized that the way her groups used *ho'oponopono* departed in some ways from what was outlined in *Nānā I Ke Kumu*, but she also acknowledged that the version of *ho'oponopono* from *Nānā I Ke Kumu*, as explained by Keola Espiritu, "feels the best and this is the one we've used." She was grateful to have the book as a resource for its clear and precise definitions, although in the program her groups have used *ho'oponopono* in a more general way.

> There isn't always a problem, which means an injurer and an injured caught in *hihia*, the net. We don't go through all the steps every time. We only go through all the steps when there is an injurer and an injured.

Virginia also had questions about who could take the role of *haku*, or leader. Initially she had Hawaiian individuals from the community lead the sessions, but after a few months when outside resource people became less available, she decided that she or her camp counselors would lead it. It was then she realized that the strength was in the process itself and not the person. This was quite a turnaround because earlier she had doubted that a non-Hawaiian could lead *ho'oponopono*.

When Virginia was asked what difficulties she encountered using *ho'oponopono,* she replied, "I don't recall any!" However, at other points in the interview she mentioned a few items of concern. She recalled that some other counselors had been resistant to using *ho'oponopono* without training. Also, she had thought that her "haoleness" might be a problem but found that problems with her different ethnic backgound didn't materialize—"I became 'Mama Virginia.'" Another area of concern involved her counselors' misunderstanding of the concept of restitution. Virginia believed that because Western society is so oriented toward "crime and punishment," some counselors equated restitution with punishment.

Virginia raised the issue of using *ho'oponopono* with cultural groups other than Hawaiians. She expressed a strong belief in its possible applications for use with non-Hawaiian groups. In her program most of the boys were "local" (i.e., had grown up in Hawaii; many were ethnically part-Hawaiian). Even those who were not of Hawaiian ethnic background shared some degree of Hawaiian cultural identification. However, she believed that *ho'oponopono* would be particularly transferable to other ethnic groups such as native Americans and Hispanics who were going through cultural identity struggles. She thought equivalent concepts probably existed in all cultures and that appropriate and corresponding terms could be used instead of the Hawaiian ones. But she emphasized that the complex process and steps should be kept intact because they were "therapeutically sound." Interestingly, she also believed the process would be most difficult with *haoles*—". . . at least ones acculturated to left-brain, cognitive values. I see *ho'oponopono* as a right-brain activity—more meditative and even mystical in how it works."

In addition, Virginia believed that varying the leadership style in *ho'oponopono* is all right. She said that the relationship of the leader to the group is perhaps most crucial. Access to supportive, authentic resource people was an implied recommendation to anyone thinking of using the process.

Robert Padua

Context of Use. Robert was born and reared in Hawaii and has strong ties with his Filipino heritage. His father is renowned on Oahu as a master of a Filipino martial art, one in which Robert is also considered well trained. He was the head counselor for Virginia Wahler's residential treatment program. His background is distinguished from the other individuals interviewed by not only his ethnicity but also his education level. Although he had not completed college, Virginia had an enormous amount of confidence in Robert's ability to act as camp manager as well as head counselor. The boys at camp responded positively to this man who taught primarily by being a positive model and espousing the simple joys of life. He demonstrated an ability to be strong and firm or sensitive and yielding, whichever was appropriate for the situation. He perceived himself to be effective because of his spiritual faith and believed he was a "channel" for powers greater than his own. The spiritual quality was an advantage he thought "counselors with M.A. degrees" often lacked.

Comments About Ho'oponopono. Whereas Virginia was the overall program director and had many tasks that kept her busy in her office, Robert's position as head counselor meant that he lived at camp with the boys. This often included weekends. His role required that he be responsible for maintaining the positive tone set by the program's goals. Each day's activities included a daily *ho'oponopono* session led by Robert. He first witnessed versions of *ho'oponopono* led by Hawaiian resource people from the community. He acknowledged that he learned a lot from these individuals but realized that what he saw wasn't really his "way" and he had doubts about its effectiveness. When Virginia made the decision that she and the camp counselors would begin leading the sessions, she taught Robert and the other counselors. The version of *ho'oponopono* they learned was from *Nānā I Ke Kumu*. During the interview Robert reached for his wallet and drew out a small, businesslike card on which the basic steps and conditions for *ho'oponopono* were neatly typed. Robert said he used it to teach the boys and to remind himself if he forgot the Hawaiian terms.

Robert identified the basic purpose of *ho'oponopono* as "problem solving."

> I don't know how other people hold their *ho'oponopono,* but our boys all came here because they had problems. And *ho'oponopono* is one of the tools to solve their problems. I don't know—I hate to say it, but some people are devilish. There's a devil in them, and it just overcomes them. It's like being possessed. And *ho'oponopono* knows this and *ho'oponopono* senses this and eliminates it. But the hard thing is, "did we do the right thing?" 'Cause our main purpose is to solve problems, not to throw away problems.

Robert agreed with Virginia that *ho'oponopono* is useful for both small and large problems. As he explained it, some of the simple problems that might arise in a session would deal with "getting up in the morning, setting the table, and being on time." During a session with these concerns the boys would often make agreements to help one another keep on schedule or follow through on an assigned task. Some of the larger problems included running away from camp, conflicts with camp staff members not associated with their program, and physical violence among the boys. When asked about some of the outcomes of these sessions, Robert said, "I used to call it small miracles because—the change in the boys—not the boys, but the leaders. The so-called negative leaders—they were so much turned around. Much softer. No shrug in the shoulders."

With each treatment group Robert saw major changes by the fourth month and said of these changes, "I knew it was *ho'oponopono* constantly being used. I think that's the fuse. I think that's the main ingredient to the changing of the boys."

Some of the specific changes that Robert attributed to *ho'oponopono* were related to relationships and values. By using the process every day, he said, "You become closer, as a family, an *'ohana*. And it becomes natural. It's just a thing that becomes love. It becomes family. You want to—I mean, I feel that the boys look forward for it."

Later in the interview Robert reiterated this point.

> When you do it constantly, you form a relationship. And this family-type relationship brings out the honesty in the individual, and in the circle, the *ho'oponopono* circle. If there is fallacy, or false, somehow it eliminates. It's a process of elimination too.

Although Robert frequently spoke glowingly of the changes in the boys and largely attributed them to *ho'oponopono,* he did admit that it was very difficult to judge how much long-term change has been achieved.

> You try to tell yourself that you did right. But did we really do right? It could have been 1 percent or 10 percent that could have been saved, but how can we judge that? So I see that *ho'oponopono* eliminates, but yet, we don't know if the person really has been saved.

As mentioned earlier Robert was skeptical at first about whether or not *ho'oponopono* was effective. He was able to see the value of the process only after using it on a daily basis and developing a leadership style that was comfortable for him. Several adaptations were made. Robert did not always use the steps as outlined because he felt that the structure did not work for him. The boys were all taught the Hawaiian terms for the steps and concepts, but in the daily sessions Robert used English terms instead. The discussions were less formal, which meant that they weren't channeled by the leader. Robert admitted, "We've made a lot of shortcuts." His main goal was to have a process that emphasized truthfulness and clear communication. He said that in the six-month period the boys are in camp, "There isn't enough time for workshops and study that would give them the 'true way of *ho'oponopono*' so *ho'oponopono* to me is—I really don't know the real truth. All I know is the way we tell it. Like the song, we did it our way, and we'll be criticized. And it shouldn't be that way. The Hawaiians will say, 'step-by-step,' but I don't know. We just felt the spirit."

Robert mentioned only a few difficulties in using ho'oponopono. He was aware that some people outside of the program seemed resistant to using the process. He saw this primarily as a fear of truth, closeness, and change. Another quite different barrier cropped up with a nonlocal *haole* boy who was in the program. He "didn't last" and left the program because the cultural context was too different from that to which he was accustomed. Like Virginia, Robert concluded there would be difficulty using ho'oponopono with nonlocal boys, although he did not elaborate on his reasons.

A definite theme throughout the talks with Robert was his personal conviction of the positive value of ho'oponopono. He affirmed that if he ever had a family of his own he would use the process. It is a process that made him feel better about himself and others. In his enthusiasm on the subject he stated, "That's the way the world should be—a big *ho'oponopono!*" Perhaps the key element in the process for him was the spiritual. Robert believed the process worked when the spiritual part is felt by the participants.

Robert's first reaction to a question asking for recommendations to others was a frank, "I really don't know." A minute later he was able to say, "It takes a lot of time, you know, to do ho'oponopono. Yeah, it will work. If you want to learn—hold it as a workshop type, yearly. But, if you want to get results. . . ."

Jean Baker

Context of Use. Jean came to Hawaii in 1976 from the midwestern region of the United States. Her education and training focused on "experiential education," which used outdoor experiences like hiking, rock climbing, and canoeing as ways to enhance physical, emotional, and intellectual growth. Another related area of interest was humanistic education and counseling. Jean has also had training in Gestalt therapy, peer counseling, and parent education programs. Some of the personal values that Jean shared during the interview included freedom, the importance of family, individuality, independence, and improving relationships with friends.

Jean was a director for a program that provided an opportunity for a wilderness experience in Hawaii. Its slogan, "You're better than you think you are," challenged individuals to explore their potential more fully by undertaking a 4- to 24-day wilderness course. The course challenged the physical, emotional, spiritual, and intellectual dimensions, giving participants an experience that might trigger a starting point, turning point, or point of reaffirmation in their lives.

One thing that distinguished this program from similar programs else-where was an emphasis on emotional growth and on positive, caring group relations. The program used the concept ʻohana to describe the group of approximately ten individuals who made the wilderness jour-ney. During the interview I asked Jean to describe how important hoʻoponopono was in the program.

> Our school is dedicated to teaching skills and it's also dedicated to maintain-ing its relation with the environment, which is Hawaii, which is Hawaiian. So it's essential that we're teaching the ethnobotany; that we're teaching the history, the legends; that we're teaching about the Hawaiian sky and the geology, and everything around you that's Hawaiian. Everything that we teach has a Hawaiian focus on it. Because that's where we are. And in the same respect, hoʻoponopono is a vital part of our program. It just links it all together. It makes us whole. It makes it all make sense that we don't have to go out and borrow some Swedish kind of problem solving to work with Hawaiian people.

Within the context of the wilderness courses, hoʻoponopono was taught to the participants, both to educate them about the Hawaiian practice and to make it an available tool for group problem solving while in the program. It was also used with the staff during instructor training and orientation.

Comments About Hoʻoponopono. Jean learned about hoʻoponopono by reading Nānā I Ke Kumu. The book was circulated among the pro-gram staff and sparked discussions about how the process might be used in the wilderness courses. Once they decided to use it, Hawaiiana experts from the community were invited to help with staff training. This gave the staff an opportunity to learn more about hoʻoponopono and to obtain some community leaders' reactions to the program's intended use of the practice. Regular staff training included communication skills and group process, which Jean saw as groundwork for competent use of hoʻoponopono.

To Jean, the literal translation of hoʻoponopono, "to make right," summed up the meaning. Furthermore, she described it as a way "to deal with any kind of problems or conflicts that come up in a group setting." Like Virginia and Robert, she also saw hoʻoponopono as valuable when used in a more general, reinforcing way. "We'll often do a lot of positive things to help keep the energy high. To acknowledge people's contribu-tions. To validate their roles."

Jean emphasized the value of using hoʻoponopono when small prob-lems occurred rather than waiting for large conflicts. In this way if the lit-tle problems were handled well, then the participants experienced feelings of success associated with the process and were more likely to request it when another problem arose.

As program director, part of Jean's responsibilities included meeting with each participant after the course ended to get a sense of what impact the course had on him or her. Jean asked whether or not the participant had done *ho'oponopono* and if it did any good. Although Jean never recorded any of the specific responses, she did have a general conclusion about them.

> People come away from the course being able to express themselves a lot better. Knowing that they can do it—they can solve problems just like they can climb to the top of a mountain. That it isn't so frightening any more to talk about a problem. And, I don't think they can go away and lead a *ho'oponopono* or that they miss it, but I think that they do miss the more intimate, the more genuine, talk about their feelings. And I think in that respect, it's very successful.

In using *ho'oponopono* in the courses, Jean recognized that there were some alterations. The course instructors reassured the participants that one traditional possible outcome, *mo ka piko,* would not be used. This phrase refers to the severance of a relationship that could occur as a consequence of an unresolved serious offense that threatened the continued harmony of the family. Harboring a grudge and being unwilling to forgive another person could precipitate the drastic measure of *mo ka piko.* Jean believed that this alternative had no place in their program.

The discussion phase was handled differently than the traditional version, since the discussion usually was not channeled through the leader. The leader would step in if expressed anger or other outbursts threatened to block problem resolution. In this case the leader's job was to reestablish a calm atmosphere and help the group understand "that they don't have to be controlled by what they're feeling. To remind them of their *aloha* that they have. And that they can solve problems." The leader might then facilitate the discussion and speak with one person at a time.

The *pani,* or closing phase of the session, did not always include a snack or meal. Instead Jean might suggest a swim in the ocean or a few minutes of individual solitude. Generally, Jean seemed to favor the continued use of *ho'oponopono,* not just in their program but wherever it might be useful. She realized that some people feared using it, and she contributed her ideas about what some of the objections might be: "We can't use *ho'oponopono* because the problem's not big enough" or "because I'm not Hawaiian" or "because we don't do it by the letter of the law, so it's not *ho'oponopono.*"

Jean's reaction to such objections was skeptical.

I personally don't buy it. I think it's an incredible and very sophisticated process and it's something that you can share with people. And that it will help the history live on. By using it, not by not using it, not by putting it in a closet until the Hawaiian race is restored, or something, because that's not likely.

This feeling of Jean's was related to something that she saw as a major barrier in the use of *hoʻoponopono*—the tendency for people to treat it as "bigger than life." Jean said, "It is just life. It's just taking care of problems. And that's an everyday thing. And when you do it, your life is richer. I think that's a very key thing for people to understand."

She believed that too reverential an attitude toward the process could create a resistance to using it. She speculated that the resistance might be due to a person's lack of confidence, knowledge, or skills. Her program attempted to overcome this barrier by creating for each course a leadership team that paired an inexperienced leader with an instructor who was more skilled. Jean saw the fear of dealing with anger as another inhibiting factor for instructors. She thought that dealing with anger was the most difficult issue in *hoʻoponopono*. However, she expressed confidence in a variety of strategies within *hoʻoponopono* that could be used to deal with the anger; these included getting rid of it by expressing it verbally or by calling a *hoʻomalu* to take the angry individual aside to allow him or her to express the anger away from the group.

Jean mentioned some minor problem areas that were mostly related to using *hoʻoponopono* within the context of a wilderness journey. For example, instructors needed to be sensitive to the energy level of the group and to avoid convening a session when the group was exhausted from a day of arduous hiking. Timing was also crucial. Instructors were to make sure that sessions did not prevent the group from being at a scheduled course destination. Practical matters, these issues were very important for the wilderness program.

When asked if she had any recommendations for those who might want to use *hoʻoponopono,* Jean said, "Just to do it. Don't let it be bigger than life. Let it be a usable thing. Give it away to people to be something that they can use. Don't hoard it."

Joseph Whitney

Context of Use. Although Joseph was born on the mainland, he moved to Hawaii when he was an infant. He has traveled quite a bit in Asia and considers living in other cultures a training experience. Joseph got his bachelor's degree in two disciplines, English and psychology, and has followed his formal education with training in humanistic psychology, group process, and communication. While talking with Joseph, I got the impression that he seeks challenging experiences, particularly those that involve learning from other cultures and traditions. In talking about personal values he mentioned his hopes for a world of trust, openness, "transparent communication" and love, and his belief in the interdependence of all things.

At the time of the interview Joseph had just returned from a trip and was preparing to leave on another. His experience using *ho'oponopono* had been with the wilderness school, working with Jean Baker and others. He worked a few summers with the school as an instructor, facilitating *ho'oponopono* sessions both with course participants and the staff.

In addition to using *ho'oponopono* with groups here in Hawaii, Joseph had used it in two other wilderness-type courses on the mainland. The groups in both courses consisted of delinquent adolescent males; one group was predominantly blacks from Pennsylvania and the other was mostly upper-class whites from Southern California. Joseph was the only individual in this study who used *ho'oponopono* outside of Hawaii.

Comments About Ho'oponopono. Joseph first encountered the concept of *ho'oponopono* while doing volunteer work with prison inmates. The way the inmates explained it to him was "everyone pulling together," which reminded Joseph of the Hawaiian concept *laulima*. Early in 1978 Joseph attended a humanistic psychology conference and met an instructor from the wilderness school. This meeting eventually led to a job with the organization. When he first began working with the wilderness program, his understanding of *ho'oponopono* was quite vague. "It was just this mystical group process that made everything all right when there was a group problem. Then I read *Nānā I Ke Kumu*. And that's where I got my understanding of it."

During the interview Joseph stated that the purpose of *ho'oponopono* was "for resolving any conflict that involves the group, not for a conflict between two people." He used it mostly as an intervention measure but said it could be considered preventive in that it kept problems from growing.

Joseph had used a variety of group problem-solving strategies but in most situations preferred to use *ho'oponopono:* "I'm in favor of *ho'oponopono* above other group processes I'm aware of, because it seems to me that other group processes can be included in *ho'oponopono*."

He listed some features *ho'oponopono* has that other group methods lack: "The prayer maybe. The solemn group agreement of 'Do you accept me as a leader? We're gonna stay with one layer of the onion.' The agreement that 'We won't enter into this unless everyone has the spirit of truth. At the end of this *ho'oponopono* there's *ho'omalu* on everything. Silence. It's dead. We won't talk about it anymore.' I really appreciate that."

As his experience using the process increased, Joseph's attitude toward it changed. He realized that *ho'oponopono* was not a cure-all and that there were some problems, particularly organizational ones, that could not be resolved in the process. However, even after this sobering realization, Joseph maintained that he still preferred to use *ho'oponopono* even when the outcome was not likely to be ideal. In the Hawaii wilderness program he thought *ho'oponopono* ". . . was very appropriate, as a forum. As a well-structured thing that guided the group process along certain lines—that I see as real valuable." He believed that most of the participants had a very positive attitude about it. "I've had students say, 'This is incredible. I wish we had more.'" More confirmation of its value came from the parents of a course participant who exclaimed to Joseph, "What's this *ho'oponopono*? My son comes back and all of a sudden he wants the family to sit down together and talk. What is this?"

When Joseph used *ho'oponopono* with the young black men on the mainland he found it to be incredibly difficult, primarily because there was so little trust in the group. Yet even after this frustrating experience, one of the toughest kids came up to Joseph after the course and said, "Hey, I really owe you," which, according to Joseph, could be roughly translated as "You're my friend."

Joseph adhered to most of the steps in *ho'oponopono* that were outlined in *Nānā I Ke Kumu*. One area of divergence was in the discussion phase. He allowed discussion directly among participants, although as a leader he channeled a lot of it. Another variation was in the use of co-leaders when a staff *ho'oponopono* was held. The series of sessions in this case lasted for three days, a time frame that would have made it very fatiguing and complex for one person to facilitate alone. When using the process on the mainland Joseph approached the use of *ho'oponopono* differently. With the blacks from Pennsylvania he spent time "talking story" about Hawaiian culture and legends and included an explanation of *ho'oponopono*. When the boys showed an interest he suggested they might use it sometime. When he finally led a *ho'oponopono* session with them he didn't use the Hawaiian terms, since they had little meaning to the boys. To these institution-wise boys the process seemed simply a variation of what they sarcastically referred to as "group."

Joseph made very little mention of his personal attitudes regarding *ho'oponopono* adaptations as being positive or negative. As a result of his experience with the mainland groups, though, he said it takes some experimentation to know when a group is ready for it. He was also convinced that there was a strong relationship between a high level of group trust and positive outcomes.

In addition to problems with low levels of trust, Joseph found that poor listening skills, inability to recognize and express feelings, and lack

of appreciation for other group members were factors that could interfere with achieving a favorable resolution in *ho'oponopono*.

Perhaps the major change in Joseph's expectations about *ho'oponopono* results came during a marathon staff session he co-led. During the
session some of the concerns individuals expressed involved organizational policies and procedures. Joseph had serious doubts about whether
or not *ho'oponopono* should be used in this type of situation, since usually management has considerably more power than staff in decision
making, thereby undermining the basic egalitarian atmosphere necessary
in *ho'oponopono*. He perceived other problems in the staff *ho'oponopono;* these included unclear group expectations of what was to be
resolved, unclear roles of participants who also had authority within the
organization, and value differences among participants. The length of
the marathon-type sessions led to what Joseph called "personal burnout"
from too much "emotional intensity." He also said he had the feeling that
even after three days the issues were not really resolved and that the sessions should have had some follow-up. In this situation Joseph concluded
that *ho'oponopono* had been used inappropriately.

His experiences led him to begin assessing groups to determine which
ones had the necessary prerequisites for *ho'oponopono*. He had now
concluded that *ho'oponopono* may not be effective in hierarchical organizations for resolving business matters. However, it may be useful for
airing concerns and interpersonal difficulties within an organization.
Another group with whom Joseph would hesitate using the process is
psychiatric patients. He also warned about being wary of "people who
want to do group all the time," since sometimes conflict is not interpersonal and can be remedied in other ways. Favorable conditions for positive results included ensuring that the *ho'oponopono* setting is comfortable, that the participants are not unduly tired, and that the process is
not bound by time limits. Finally, he stated that leading *ho'oponopono* is
a skill that required a "nonjudgmental attitude, real warm and real
accepting, assertive—being aware of (your) own energy level." Joseph
found it helpful to prepare himself by spending time alone before leading
a session.

Joseph's suggestion to people who are considering using *ho'oponopono* was:

> If you've only heard about it, sit in on half a dozen first. Be pretty clear
> when you're gonna' do it. Summon up all the *aloha* and all the support you
> can, from wherever you get it. And, just don't be afraid, I mean, just go past
> it. 'Cause it's a really scary thing to lead one. And, I would say too, don't,
> don't get caught up in, "Was it a good or bad *ho'oponopono?*" I think
> they're all worthy *ho'oponopono*s.

Joseph had one other strongly held belief he wanted to share about *ho'oponopono*.

I think, for me, one of the most wonderful aspects about it is that it's so connected with, say, with these islands, with this culture. That it comes out of such an interconnectedness. And it can teach a lot besides communication, and I think that's really necessary these days.

Paul Ellis

Context of Use. Paul, who was reared in Chicago, has lived in Hawaii for about ten years. He seemed to be an intense, hardworking person with a playful sense of humor, characterized by his assertion that his ethnic background was "green-eyed devil."

His educational interests have been in social theory and "conflict." He has had human relations training, including encounter group models, and for a while worked with a national group that provided training for business and educational organizations.

Although he has a Ph.D. in sociology, he claimed that he was most at home outdoors. "I feel very connected with the natural world—that's where I feel most in place."

He combined his love of the natural environment with his work while he was an instructor in the wilderness program. Jean, Joseph, and Paul worked together in this organization for a few summers.

At the time of the interview, Paul was executive director of a burgeoning center in Honolulu. Set up to mediate disputes, the center offers an alternative to litigation for individuals who would prefer to settle disagreements outside of a court of law. Paul gave me a center brochure that had the word *ho'oponopono* on the front. The use of this concept was designed to illustrate the similarities between mediation and the practice of *ho'oponopono*. Another section of the brochure explained that the opening of the center "brings to Hawaii a new way of resolving disputes but at the same time it is also a return to an old way; the traditional Hawaiian way of *ho'oponopono;* a way of resolving disputes by talking them out in the family or extended family setting in the spirit of *'ohana* and *aloha*."

Although the *ho'oponopono* concept may set a Hawaiian tone for mediation, the process itself, with one or two exceptions, has not been used to settle disputes. The interview with Paul was primarily based on his use of *ho'oponopono* while he worked in the wilderness program, but some of his ideas and recommendations about potential uses for *ho'oponopono* arose from his new work in dispute settlement.

Comments About Ho'oponopono. As with the other wilderness course instructors, Paul's major introduction to *ho'oponopono* came when he began to work for the program, since leading sessions was part of an instructor's responsibility. The instructors were each given a program manual that included a brief description of *ho'oponopono* as explained in *Nānā I Ke Kumu*. The description essentially provided a list of terms and their definitions.

During the interview, Paul distinguished between the purposes of *ho'oponopono* in the past and in the present. He believed that in the past it was "the very core of keeping an *'ohana* together," whereas today it functions as "a method by which people deepen relationships." But he saw a similarity between *ho'oponopono*'s use in the past and its use in the wilderness courses. "When you have a group that constituted itself as an *'ohana* and would be traveling through the wilderness for 24 days, you really became kind of a family." Paul also perceived two other dimensions of *ho'oponopono* during sessions with the staff.

> Sometimes they were used as a way of trying to clarify interpersonal issues, and some of the sessions were kind of focusing on particular individuals who were experiencing a lot of pain. Both dimensions I saw—sort of a therapeutic dimension and the other was sort of the problem solving. That's one of the things that struck me about it—was the power of it. That it could do both of those kinds of things. That it was sort of a combination of psychotherapy plus a social problem-solving mechanism that I've never seen anyplace else. And I've never experienced it with so much intensity. And I have a little experience with some counseling strategies and that kind of thing, so I was swept up into this and very much enchanted with it and it became kind of the portal, the doorway for me to look into Hawaiian culture with a lot more depth than I had at that time.

Paul also made the distinction that *ho'oponopono* was used for group difficulties rather than individual ones. He saw its function as a method of conflict intervention or, if used regularly, conflict prevention.

According to Paul, the degree of group relatedness was a key factor in the effectiveness of a *ho'oponopono* session. He believed that in the wilderness courses the participants were related by a common experience. "So I think *ho'oponopono* was very appropriate for this. Because it was an *'ohana*, not by blood, but by the very virtue of experience. They were a family for 24 days. For better or for worse, they were related to one another."

Like Joseph, Paul concluded that there were limitations to the use of the process.

> I think one of the misunderstandings that a lot of people (in the wilderness course) got into was that *ho'oponopono* could do miracles in terms of kind of taking some organizational problems that were in existence and changing

those. And I think what's been learned is that there was kind of a belief that *ho'oponopono* could do almost anything. You know, "any kind of problem —bring it on—we'll solve it." We could get the prisoners out of Iran if we could just get the chance to sit them down! What I realized also is that *ho'oponopono* had limitations. That you could address interpersonal problems with it and resolve those kinds of things, but that there were kinda' class problems—I don't know how to describe it—organizational problems and power problems that couldn't be resolved through *ho'oponopono*.

These limitations have not diminished Paul's enthusiasm for the process. He cited examples of positive changes in the wilderness course group after *ho'oponopono* sessions, even when they had not been able to go through a formal resolution process. Also, he was examining it to see what might be applicable for mediation.

Paul specified a few ways that he diverged from the traditional process. He was not always able to get the participants to express a formal apology. Also, instead of channeling the discussion, he encouraged participants to talk directly to one another. Sometimes rather than preventing emotional outbursts or interruptions he let them occur. "You've got to let people have their dispute. People are there to have a fight and you're not there to squelch it and squash it." When things did appear to be getting out of hand, Paul used the cooling-off time, *ho'omalu,* both in *ho'oponopono* sessions and in mediation.

I don't pretend that what we do is the way it was done a hundred years ago. But then again I don't know if anyone's pretending that these days. It's sort of transmuted. It's adapted. It's taken new shape. It's a real protean concept anyway that should evolve in its own direction.

Later during the interview we discussed various reactions in the community to *ho'oponopono* adaptations and wondered who should make decisions about its use. He responded:

Well, I don't think anybody should. I mean, I don't think anybody can— even Kawena [Pukui]. I take it as a source. See, it's such a living thing for me. I mean I really think it's such a neat, living thing that can be used and should be tried in lots of different ways. And I'm gonna' continue to do that.

Generally Paul seemed to favor making *ho'oponopono* accessible for families and groups. As mentioned earlier, he looked at *ho'oponopono* to see what he could learn about making mediation more effective. He believed mediation and *ho'oponopono* had similar objectives.

To heal relationships. To take relationships that are strained, for whatever reason, and to begin uncovering the various layers of guck and gunk and

garbage that is there, and to peel some of that stuff back and try and heal.
Heal the relationships. Like doctors heal the body, in meditation you heal
the soul, and in mediation you're healing relationships between people, so
that the outcome potentially is very similar.

Paul mentioned that he had used ho'oponopono with two cases at the
mediation center. One instance involved a divorced Hawaiian couple
who needed to work out the husband's visitation rights. Rather than
using the process in its entirety, Paul invoked the spirit of ho'oponopono,
which gave the discussions that followed a serious quality in terms both
familiar and meaningful to the couple. Another time he used it with a
young Hawaiian couple and it did not work. They did not know about
the concept so it had no special significance. In the future Paul is anxious
to explore the possible use of ho'oponopono with child custody cases.

Paul appeared to be cautious about using ho'oponopono in mediation.
One of the dilemmas for him involved its spiritual element. Paul saw the
practice as being more secular today than in the past, yet also acknowledged that the spiritual element was crucial. He believed that the haku
should have firm spiritual beliefs. When mediation and ho'oponopono
were compared he saw a qualitative difference between the two.

> That's one of the differences between mediation and ho'oponopono. I just
> realized that mediation is very much of a tool, and the question ultimately
> is, "Does it work?" or "Does it not work?" Ho'oponopono in my mind is a
> tool, but it's also a philosophy—so I've kinda' got ho'oponopono on a
> slightly different level.

Paul had a few concerns about ho'oponopono, some of which have
been mentioned earlier. He thought that certain groups of people lacked
a sufficient degree of interdependence for the successful use of ho'oponopono. He listed some examples of groups for which the process might be
inappropriate: a city council, work colleagues, or people who are not
from or familiar with Hawaii. An example given for the latter was
"blacks from Chicago." He believed organizational problems did not lend
themselves to resolution by use of ho'oponopono. He also warned of
"ho'oponopono junkies," those people who love to be involved in group
process to an extreme degree. Another potential problem could arise if
the leader was a haole and the group was Hawaiian. This situation once
confronted a friend of Paul's. The group was initially very suspicious of
the leader but eventually accepted him. Paul also told of a situation
where an individual wanted to do ho'oponopono, but the others were
not ready. "The spirit wasn't right." When this happened, Paul waited
and scheduled it when the timing was right for the whole group.

Paul's suggestions to anyone who might use *ho'oponopono* in the future included reading everything possible on the subject and talking to as many resource people as possible. Additional advice was, "Get clear on why you want to do it and what you're gonna' do with it."

Keola Espiritu

Context of Use. Keola is a central figure in this study. He appeared in chapter 1 as the young social worker whose work with a case involving Hawaiian illness put into motion a series of events that led to the formation of the Culture Committee and eventually the publication of *Nānā I Ke Kumu.*

Keola was born in Hawaii of Hawaiian-Filipino parentage, although his socialization was primarily Hawaiian. The family's home was in a rural area of windward Oahu. In college Keola was keenly interested in anthropology, which gave him a scientific basis for understanding culture and complemented his experience of being reared in a household that had strong Hawaiian cultural beliefs and practices. He also obtained a master's degree in social work. His first job as a social worker was with a Hawaiian agency. Later he began a public service career. He has continued to expand his knowledge about Hawaiian culture, has served on a commission for historic preservation, and is renowned as a Hawaiiana expert. Keola takes great personal pride and enjoyment in his family. On weekends he can often be found working and playing with family and friends—singing, fishing, or hiking in the hills behind his house.

Keola's use of *ho'oponopono* resulted from his personal interest in the process and had not been under the auspices of any particular program. Because of this, Keola has had extensive experience using *ho'oponopono* in a variety of contexts. In addition to using the process in social work practice with Hawaiian families, he has used it in the following settings: with members of his *hui* (community group or club), with employees in his office, with the crew on a boating expedition, with couples or families of various ethnic backgrounds, and with his own family. The problems discussed ranged widely and included land and housing disputes, personal crises, unsatisfactory employee relations, lack of trust among group members, ramifications of psychiatric difficulties, and a normal host of marital and family upsets.

Comments About Ho'oponopono. Since the section on "Reemergence of Ho'oponopono" in chapter 1 explained how Keola learned about *ho'oponopono,* the information will not be repeated. Suffice it to say that Keola's primary source of information was Pukui and the work of the QLCC Culture Committee.

Keola articulated what he believed to be the three aspects of *ho'oponopono* use: diagnostic, remedial, and preventive. He explained that these three aspects also formed a sequence of possible outcomes of *ho'oponopono*. The first, diagnostic, gives a group the opportunity to air feelings and identify a problem so that everyone knows where the responsibilities lie. If the group is not ready or willing to proceed through the resolution phase of the process, then the *ho'oponopono* could be labeled "diagnostic." Keola believed this was a legitimate and worthwhile outcome. The second aspect is remedial and occurs when the problem is identified, and the group proceeds to rectify the situation through forgiveness and restitution. The ideal outcome is preventive. Sessions serve a preventive function when the group holds *ho'oponopono* on a regular basis even when there are no obvious problems. Keola acknowledged he has done this with his family.

> We do it in the sense of saying, "Hey, let's get together for—"; you sense something's going on, but nobody's saying anything and something's amiss. "Hey, let's get together and let's talk—talk story." And in that talking story you find out that there are problems. So it's preventive in the sense that it hasn't blown up sky high, but it's there.

Aside from articulating the three uses of *ho'oponopono,* Keola had another idea about the purpose. He believed that one of the aims in the process was to encourage people to act in a responsible way.

> One of the values of *ho'oponopono* is to get people to behave in an adult, mature way. O.K., when I say "mature" I mean age-appropriate. Because in so doing, by them being in control, then they'll be responsible for what they're saying. But if the immaturity comes through—"I'm not gonna' be responsible for what I'm saying"—then that creates problems.

Like some of the other individuals in the case studies, Keola favors using *ho'oponopono* as the method of choice when working with groups "because I've found it works." Keola shared another reason for feeling most comfortable using the process.

> I've found out, too, that if you use it you can always check yourself. Where you went astray, or where the group went astray. Because there's a set process, and the process will elicit—it's like a flow chart. A flow chart that if it's "yes" this is what you do. If it's "no" this is what you do. And I find that people are readily able to participate because it's concrete to them. They can repeat it, so hopefully after you're through with the process they pretty much can do it themselves. Or are willing to try. So I find that from experience-wise, I find it's a good, good learning experience for the group itself, as well as for the therapist. It becomes easier too.

Keola used behavioral assessments to determine what the outcome of the sessions had been. In the case with the delinquent boy mentioned in chapter 1, the boy's return to school was a positive indication. In another case he and his wife led sessions with a man who had a history of hospitalization for occasional psychotic episodes; cessation of the need for hospitalization after *ho'oponopono* provided the indication of success.

During the sessions Keola relied on his feelings to determine whether or not sincere and deep resolution had taken place. During the resolution phase when individuals ask for forgiveness and release, Keola often saw deep emotions expressed. If this did not occur it signaled him that the problems may not have been fully uncovered and discussed. Then Keola would return to the discussion phase of the process until the issues had been more fully explored and all participants showed their readiness to move through the forgiveness and release phase.

One part of the process that Keola modified was the prayer. Traditionally prayers were offered to the *'aumākua,* the four major gods, or the multiple gods. In his personalized *pule,* Keola substituted "powers that be" for the gods and believed that this change was in keeping with the essence that was traditionally intended.

When Keola first began to use *ho'oponopono,* he saw it as a method to be used only with Hawaiian members of an *'ohana.* Later he branched out and used it with other ethnic groups and with nonfamily groups. He said he has learned not to assume that the group, even if Hawaiian, understands or values the Hawaiian terms or formal ritual of the process; he used English terms when they seem most appropriate. "The reason for this is that in any treatment process where communication is important, the communicaton has to be in the language everybody will understand."

Keola also has altered the role of the *haku* to fit various situations. In one instance, when he was with a group of friends from his *hui,* one friend became embroiled in a conflict and became uncomfortably vulnerable in the process. Keola and a few others in the *hui* who were social workers familiar with *ho'oponopono* began to use *ho'oponopono*-type strategies to alleviate the person's stress. They did this without identifying or utilizing a formal *haku.* In working with other groups, particularly couples with marital problems, Keola shared the role of the *haku* with his wife Lani, who is also featured in the case studies. When Keola worked with a family over a period of time and the family members became familiar with the process, he said he found himself playing a less active role as leader. Eventually the *haku* role was turned over to a person in the family and Keola functioned more as a resource person.

Keola identified another modification during the *mihi, kala,* and *oki* stage. Traditionally all discussions were channeled through the leader, even during the forgiveness and release stage. However, Keola has found that this was often a time when positive expressions of concern, such as hugging and kissing, and heartfelt apologies were likely to occur. So he encouraged these expressions to be communicated directly from one individual to another rather than to be channeled through the leader.

Since Keola's experiences using *ho'oponopono* with various groups had been satisfying he saw a potential for it being used more widely.

> In terms of use, Lani and I have always maintained—take away the Hawaiian terminology, use the English, and you find it's not as strange or as weird. As a matter of fact, it makes good mental health practice—that with non-Hawaiians it could be utilized. And, that people—if they understood it—would be able to engage.

Keola has heard of people in the community who are using *ho'oponopono* in programs and he is supportive of their attempts.

> The position we take though is, if it works, it works, whether or not they're following the same procedure that Tūtū Pukui has outlined—a set format or not. The main thing is the problem, and there's a resolution of that problem. And if the resolution of the problem sticks and all the parties feel that they've accomplished something and they can abide by the decision, then. . . .

Keola mentioned a few concerns about problems that could arise during *ho'oponopono*. He said that the use of drugs or alcohol by participants could thwart problem resolution and advised against proceeding under these conditions. It is also important for the leader to be in control of the situation. "It has to be a situation where there is minimum interference." This included preventing excessive noise and potential disruptions by persons who are not involved directly in the *ho'oponopono* but are present on the outskirts. He recommended that those individuals should not be in the vicinity.

Keola's suggestions reinforced concerns that have been mentioned elsewhere. He was anxious for *ho'oponopono* practice to be more widely used, but he perceived a lack of adequate resources for people who were genuinely interested.

> I think there needs to be more and more of this kind of discussion. Comparison of notes of people that are doing it. And to see what kind of impact it had on what kind of problems they've had. And how they are moving.

He gave credit to those individuals who have gone ahead and tried to use the practice.

So in terms of people getting involved—my hat's off to 'em. True, there's gonna' be problems. There's no such thing as *ho'oponopono* without any problems. But the point is, they do it and they're open for learning. I think the problem is, can someone be there as a resource to kinda' explain? That's where I find the problem.

This wish for greater utilization of *ho'oponopono* was especially strong when Keola reflected on the reluctance of Hawaiians who know the process to use it. One of the last remarks of the interview summed up his feelings. With an expression that had a hint of frustration, as well as encouragement, Keola said, laughingly, "So now, move! *Hele on!*" ("Lets go!")

Kalau Souza

Context of Use. Kalau was born and reared in Hawaii and is ethnically part-Hawaiian. Throughout the interviews she told rich stories about her family, friends, and work and demonstrated considerable knowledge about Hawaiian beliefs and practices.

She has a graduate degree in social work and is professionally viewed as knowledgeable about Hawaiian culture. At the time of the interview Kalau rarely worked directly with families; most of her use of *ho'oponopono* took place a few years ago. She has used the complete process with only a few Hawaiian families, although she feels her natural style of working with families is very akin to *ho'oponopono*. In the agency where she worked Kalau said that a few other social workers approached the use of *ho'oponopono* similarly by "using certain parts of the concept as we worked. Some of it might have been unconscious, and then as we got more skilled, using the whole thing." She also acknowledged that her training in social work had been helpful in using the process and understanding the concepts.

Comments About Ho'oponopono. Kalau's primary source of information about *ho'oponopono* was from Pukui. As she learned more about *ho'oponopono* from other resources she realized that not everyone shared the same definitions.

You can talk to other Hawaiians and they will say, "We do *ho'oponopono*." And it is a simple straightening out of maybe a disagreement between two people, or two relatives, or two kids. And, it ends very often with each apologizing for the *pilikia*. And each agreeing to make restitution, or correction, or whatever else has to be done. And I guess that's one simple form of *ho'oponopono*. So it's straightening out of anything that lies between two people.

Kalau believed, "The goal for the Hawaiian is to have his family operating as a unit in harmony." So she perceived the purpose of *ho'oponopono* as the way to strive toward that goal.

> I would say *ho'oponopono* irons out difficulties in the family so that it can be a cooperative unit. This requirement of harmony was essential to our people's survival. Hence in any kind of endeavor—whether fishing, working the taro patch, building a house or in the mountains—the family in their laboring could not be distracted by family worries, as this could cause accidents with serious results.

She thought *ho'oponopono* could be used as prevention to keep problems from getting larger or as intervention to resolve an acute problem. Aside from the goal of maintaining family unity, Kalau conceived that it could also be a way for a troubled couple to look honestly at their relationship to determine whether or not they should stay together. In cases where *ho'oponopono* might lead to a couple's decision to end their marriage, she said the process could provide a forum for making agreements about what their behavior would be toward one another in the future.

Kalau basically thought *ho'oponopono* "would work for anyone who was interested and wanted to use the practice. But it requires a commitment—to sit through it and sincerely participate." It was relating to this area of commitment that Kalau seemed to have questions about *ho'oponopono* use today. She wondered if changes in cultural beliefs and practices, particularly as they have affected the family, made it more difficult to use the practice.

> The problem I've found in working with it in today's world is that so often the kids have basketball. Another kid, he's just found a job. And, you know, there's just always some other kind of priority.

So before making a decision to use *ho'oponopono* with a family, Kalau usually spent a great deal of time developing a relationship with the group, "to get their recognition of their having a problem and wanting to work on it. They're not ready to move into anything like *ho'oponopono* until they have enough understanding of the concept and trust built." If the necessary trust had developed and the family had made the necessary agreements to meet, then Kalau proceeded. If the family could not reach an agreement to proceed with formal *ho'oponopono,* that indicated to her that another leader might be more compatible, or that the family was not ready to resolve the problem. Even after initiating formal *ho'oponopono* Kalau believed it was important to continue nurturing a close relationship with the family. She emphasized this numerous times and gave examples of how she reinforced this relationship. She made phone calls to the family between sessions just to say hello and see how they were doing. Another way was by gently easing into the discussion of problems whenever a problem-solving session began.

> I always used a warmup period too, you know, where you get caught up on news of the family and how things are. And that's what I call the warm-up. It's not to get into any of the problem situation, but to kinda feel like—like you know one another again. There's been an absence, a lack of contact, perhaps. And you don't go directly into things. So, to me, that's a very important part of the process, called *kūkulu-kumuhana*.

One of the dilemmas Kalau saw in using *ho'oponopono* with various groups was that the value orientations might be very different. As mentioned earlier, Kalau felt that family unity was the primary goal for the traditional Hawaiians who used *ho'oponopono*. However, with the Hawaiian families who have embraced Western-type value orientations that put more emphasis on an individual's concerns and needs, Kalau has found it more difficult to assess the outcome of *ho'oponopono*.

> I tried using it with a Hawaiian family that was very Westernly oriented—I don't know what was going on in their minds during the process—it still came out with, it seemed to me, everybody looking after their own territory and not really thinking of the total.

When I asked Kalau if she thought that a primary group orientation was an important prerequisite value for people participating in *ho'oponopono,* she replied, "Oh no! Well, I think—that's why I have such a hard time putting *ho'oponopono* with someone who's so 'Western oriented.' "

Kalau's adaptations of *ho'oponopono* differed from other individuals in the case studies since she had used the process only with families identified as Hawaiian. When asked if she used all the steps of the process as outlined in *Nānā I Ke Kumu*, she replied, "Well, they don't flow like that. No." The first time she used *ho'oponopono* it emerged rather spontaneously while working with a mother and her daughter. Later she used the process with the whole family more formally and educated the family about the process by using visual aids outlining the steps. In the only other adaptation specifically mentioned, Kalau sometimes used only parts of the process rather than the complete form. Kalau had not used the process in a wide variety of contexts and did not specifically state her attitudes toward the various adaptations. She acknowledged that many similarities were evident between concepts in *ho'oponopono* and concepts from Western mental health practices. However, she seemed to have some unresolved questions about the appropriateness of *ho'oponopono* for non-Hawaiians, particularly because of the many value differences. Another reason for her questions was her lack of experience using *ho'oponopono* with Western families.

> Actually the *mahiki* part is something you do as a Western practitioner, which is unpeeling of the onion. Or finding out what the problem is. What the layers are. You know it's not so different. But, I think the values that the Hawaiians have—the sincerity, the commitment—are all very essential to the whole thing.

The major difficulties that Kalau saw in using *ho'oponopono* today involved using it with families whose values and practices were greatly different from the traditional Hawaiian ones woven into *ho'oponopono*.

Kalau gave a few examples. In the past when a problem was solved a *ho'omalu* was called. "Those problems are supposed to be *pau*. You don't give it the dignity of life by repeating it." This puts a lid on further discussions of the topic. But Kalau was not sure that the power of *pau* is as valued today even when requested by an elder. Another difficulty was that many families have a mixture of Hawaiian and Western values that need to be untangled, because the value mix can cause a breakdown of communication and understanding. This may also make it difficult to maintain the order and control that is necessary in *ho'oponopono*. Perhaps the problem that Kalau found most vexing when working with families was getting them all together at one time. When a family member was missing, it seemed to her that the group got stuck, since it invariably turned out that they needed the missing person's input.

> It tells you that in the book—that you cannot. . . . Without that person you'll always find that there are blocks. So for that person not to be included is like excluding him, you see? He misses the, the repartee, if you want. And he misses his fair share. And the more you have of that, then the more you're shoving him out. You notice I said "you're." *You're* shoving him out. In a sense he's trying to get away from it all, but you're also participating.

The primary issue Kalau raised during the interview involved seeing *ho'oponopono* as something that specifically highlighted and reinforced Hawaiian values and practices. Therefore, in a rapidly changing society where Hawaiians and others mixed and altered their cultural practices, questions were raised about the purpose of *ho'oponopono* and with whom it could be used. Kalau thought it could be used with non-Hawaiians.

But to me, you know, our values are so different, in a way. At least my understanding for the Hawaiians—the goal would be to try and keep the family together. And to try and understand how the family functions—which is the working together, always working together.

Lani Espiritu

Context of Use. Lani is another central figure in this study. Keola Espiritu is her husband; with him, she was involved in the Culture Committee.

Lani was born and reared on Oahu and is part-Hawaiian. Her family had strong Hawaiian traditions, and as she grew up she participated in activities like traditional *hula*. Her training in *hula* reinforced many Hawaiian beliefs and values that later helped her understand and utilize *ho'oponopono*. Lani loves to sing and play the *'ukulele* and has done so professionally.

When she completed a master's degree in social work, she went to work for a Hawaiian social welfare agency. In addition to doing direct casework with families, Lani's professional activities have included teaching at the community college and university levels, doing research, acting as a cultural consultant for many programs, and coordinating a Pacific Islands social work project.

Like Keola, Lani beamed when she spoke of her family. She was especially proud that her children were showing great pride and interest in their Hawaiian heritage and demonstrating their skills in gathering food, fishing, and preparing for family *lū'aus*. One child has even led family *ho'oponopono* sessions.

Lani is probably the most experienced leader of *ho'oponopono* in Hawaii. She has used it with a wide range of groups although initially only with Hawaiian families. Later, as she began to resolve some of her doubts about its applicability to other groups, she began to experiment. She has used *ho'oponopono* with non-Hawaiians and unrelated groups including her agency co-workers, her students, and three families. At times, her job responsibilities have specified that she use *ho'oponopono* with Hawaiian families. In other instances she used it when requested by individuals or families.

Comments About Ho'oponopono. Lani first learned of *ho'oponopono* through the work of the QLCC Culture Committee. Pukui's explanation of the process intrigued her.

Because basically for me it was ringing bells, along the kind of things that I had done with my folks but had never had a label for. It was the kind of process where we could talk about anything and everything. So things spilled out. And you would always feel that there would be a sense of closure, of having gotten your questions answered and directions given.

At the time Lani was learning from Pukui she was also working on a case that involved many "Hawaiian" mental health issues. The mother in a family had received psychiatric assistance, including chemotherapy, for some time before Lani met her. She told Lani that she had repeatedly dreamed of her deceased grandmother. The grandmother had led many *ho'oponopono* sessions when she was alive. When Lani learned this she saw an opportunity to apply the practice of *ho'oponopono*. She told the women, "I don't know how to do it. We may have to do it in a style that is different from Grandma's. So, are you willing to try? We can learn together." This was a breakthrough for Lani as a new step in learning about *ho'oponopono*. The sessions that followed were also a therapeutic turning point for Lani's client.

Later when Lani did a project designed to test the use of *ho'oponopono* with Hawaiian families during a one-year period, she utilized a consultation team that included a psychiatrist and a cultural resource person. This culture consultancy was especially important and greatly increased her understanding.

> I could make a case presentation and really focus on me the practitioner, me the worker. Get help in regards to where I am. Where my belief system is. Where my biases are. At the same time get a perspective on the dynamics of what was happening. The pros for this kind of approach are tremendous for someone who is trying to do something new.

Lani also established an advisory board of university, private, and public agency professionals who helped her become more cognizant of the actual treatment process she was utilizing. Her skill developed through experience—"On-the-job training—with me trying it out, coming back, checking it out, doing it, coming back. That constant kind of thing."

Lani specified three purposes for which *ho'oponopono* can be used.

> One is that it gives you a good assessment of the people, in the situation—an idea of the complexity of the situation itself. An idea as to who's involved, at what level. What their behavior patterns are. Who is bounded into a problem and who is ready to move.
>
> Second, it's also corrective. Where a situation needs to be modified. Where there needs to be a remedial action. *Ho'oponopono* provides a method by which people can resolve problems and move in new directions. And these generally make for happy endings.
>
> The third purpose is one of the preventive nature. Prevention is being able to utilize whatever skills and abilities you have so that it can prevent further

breakdown of the family. It prevents more serious complications and compounding of problem areas. It doesn't mean that *ho'oponopono* wipes out all problems. It just means that it can prevent further disruption, further seriousness of the problem.

Throughout the interview Lani expressed such overwhelming enthusiasm for *ho'oponopono* that I asked her on what the enthusiasm was based. "Oh, I'm definitely convinced. I've seen the results with other families. And I've seen dramatic changes." Lani, like a few other individuals in the case studies, concluded that *ho'oponopono* was her method of choice for group problem solving. She described some of the specific changes in families and individuals. In the case with the woman who had the dreams about her grandmother, after one and a half years the woman was able to discontinue chemotherapy. The woman's mental health worker reported to Lani that there had been significant improvement, which later resulted in the case being closed by the clinic.

Lani first recognized the potential of *ho'oponopono* as a preventive process when the father in a family with which she had worked many months began to exert his skills as a leader and problem-solver in his community. Although he had not been aware that he was using *ho'o-ponopono,* he had in fact transferred his family experiences with *ho'oponopono* to his community involvement. In another case, a couple worked through fifteen years of marital difficulties in a single marathon-like *ho'oponopono* session, going back to some original problems that had festered all those years. The result was their decision to remain married, and they had a few years of an improved marriage before the husband died.

Lani and her husband once led a *ho'oponopono* with three families, including their own. The session was scheduled because two boys from the other families had burglarized the Espiritu home. Seventy-five percent of the stolen items were returned before the *ho'oponopono,* and after the session the boys made further restitution by doing yard work. Lani was especially pleased with the situation's outcome.

> With the two youngsters, it just allowed for more of the positive vibrations to come together. And I see that as a happy ending—the harmony restored. There is increased improved interpersonal relationships between the parties. And there's a deeper sense of "I care for you and you care for me 'cause we're gonna' look after each other."

Not all the cases ended with storybook happy endings, but Lani believed that having ideal outcomes should not be the only expectation of *ho'oponopono* anyway. The aim was to identify the problem and move toward resolution. Even traditional Hawaiians had the mechanism of *mo ka piko* as an alternative when harmonious relationships could not be reestablished. Lani and Keola once worked with a non-Hawaiian couple who were moving toward dissolution of their marriage.

> I think it illustrates in this case how the outcome might not be ideal. I think
> in this case it would illustrate that one can sever the structural ties of a rela-
> tionship, but that through *ho'oponopono* you can still maintain dignity and
> worth of the other individual, without being hostile. And as we're going
> through these sessions I see this as a possibility.

Lani gave one other example of using *ho'oponopono* with a group that was unable to go through reconciliation. It was with a large group of thirty unrelated people. The group did not want to proceed through the *mihi, kala,* and *oki* because they had doubts about the sincerity of some individuals. As a result part of the group boycotted the next session. Lani and Keola then explained to the remaining individuals that it was impossible to proceed. The benefits from *ho'oponopono* in this instance derived from giving the group a complete picture of the problem and its dynamics.

Lani felt that she has benefited greatly from the challenges of using *ho'oponopono* with the varied groups. "In the process of confronting and making these decisions, I think it's developed me even more. *Ho'oponopono* forced me to come to grips with what I am, who I am, what I can do, what I want to do."

She also recounted the benefits of using *ho'oponopono* with her family. One of her children is now able to lead the sessions and is regarded as a natural leader by her friends, siblings, and cousins.

When Lani first began using *ho'oponopono,* she understood it as a process that should be used only with related Hawaiians and led only by a Hawaiian. Gradually she found herself moving beyond these requirements and realized that it could work with non-Hawaiians and unrelated groups and be led by a non-Hawaiian. As her confidence and understanding of the process grew, she also began making modifications in the form but always with an eye on maintaining what she believed was the essence of *ho'oponopono.*

Some of the first modifications Lani made were attitudinal ones. Aside from the issues of Hawaiian versus non-Hawaiian and related versus unrelated, she realized that assessment and prevention were two worthy purposes of *ho'oponopono* in addition to the widely accepted one, problem resolution. Lani deviated from using the Hawaiian terms or formal ritual if it seemed to have no special meaning for the group. I asked if she would continue to call it *ho'oponopono* in these cases and she replied, "I have no need to call it *ho'oponopono.*"

A number of other adaptations involved the role of *haku*. Lani and Keola found that using co-leaders was often very effective, particularly in a marital case where individuals might feel more comfortable speaking to a person of the same sex. Also, in two situations Lani was *haku* even though she was involved in the problem. In both cases she believed that she presented her feelings on the problem without jeopardizing the essential facilitative function of the leader.

Two other changes were related to the role of *haku* and to a value Lani held about expressing emotions. Traditionally, *ho'oponopono* discouraged acting out any emotions, especially negative ones, but Lani believed that allowing individuals to express positive emotions could be helpful. During the forgiveness stage—the *mihi, kala,* and *oki*—Lani has allowed participants to talk directly to one another rather than through her. Like Keola, she encouraged a group to assume more responsibility if the members were familiar with the process of *ho'oponopono* and abided by the general procedures. "I see myself being active initially so they get a sense of *ho'oponopono,* and weaving myself out with less participation."

Another issue arose from Lani's understanding of *ho'omalu,* which includes the rules for confidentiality in the group. One day in a culture consultation at the Hawaiian agency, the psychiatrist asked Lani why she did not call *ho'omalu* after every session. She replied, "It makes a lot of sense for families in *ho'oponopono* to have a sense of resolution. They know the process. Why prevent them from discussing it? It's positive. In my mind I'm clear. It's when there's a potential for the negative entanglements to be produced, then that's what *ho'oponopono* tries to prevent."

After talking about these changes Lani laughed and exclaimed, "You know what? I'm beginning to realize that some parts of *ho'oponopono* are really Lani Espiritu style!"

When Lani talked about problems or barriers using *ho'oponopono,* some were related to the difficulty of learning the process and feeling confident as a leader. Before she decided to do the year-long *ho'oponopono* project, she went through a process of "checking out" both her personal and cultural backgrounds to determine if any factors might suggest she was unsuited to lead *ho'oponopono.* Going through this process was an important step for Lani. She recounted a story of getting a cultural validation for her work not only from her living relatives but also from her ancestors, through a message from the family *'aumakua.* The message from the *'aumakua* was revealed while Lani's mother was in an involuntary trance state (*noho,* possession). This experience was a culturally meaningful expression of validation for Lani and gave her added confidence to proceed with her *ho'oponopono* work. Lani thought that the inability of some people to validate or legitimize themselves as *ho'oponopono* leaders was a barrier to its use. She thought that this might explain why many people who know how to do *ho'oponopono* do not use it.

When Lani first used the process she sometimes got stuck and did not know how to proceed in the traditional manner. Rather than allowing this to interfere with the therapeutic process, she switched back and forth to Western intervention methods. Later she brought these matters to her consultation group or advisory committee to see how the *ho'oponopono* steps could have been used in the situation.

Another problem area she mentioned had to do with the relationships among the group members and the level of trust involved.

> It *(ho'oponopono)* requires honesty, openness, being able to put things above board. If people cannot be interdependent and extend themselves, then it's only a one-sided affair and you don't have the makings of *ho'oponopono*. That to me is a critical point. If I find that people have the ability to do this, but for some reason something has interfered with the basic sense of trust, I'd be willing to go along and risk it and say, "Trust me. Because I'm there. I have the controls necessary to make it out so that everybody is treated with dignity, respect, and fairness."

There are certain other factors that might indicate that the use of *ho'oponopono* would not be suitable. If participants were under the influence of drugs or alcohol, Lani advised against proceeding. Or if the participants had a businesslike relationship, such as a landlord and a tenant, they might not feel sufficiently interdependent to follow through the entire *ho'oponopono* process. Finally, Lani added that when participants were hesitant to proceed, it was an indication that part of the problem had not been adequately discussed.

When Lani and I discussed other potential audiences for *ho'oponopono,* she suggested that it would be helpful in a family with a foster child. Often in such a situation, adjustment is difficult for both the child and the family members. *Ho'oponopono* could be a therapeutic counseling method conducted right in the home. Lani said, "It gives kids a sense of what family living is all about."

Perhaps Lani's main concern was getting more individuals trained to do *ho'oponopono*. This had become her personal goal, something she would like to be involved with in the future. She felt that what has been written or presented in lectures has not been enough.

> My commitment goes beyond that—to get people who will provide services to families who want it and need it, to make it a living contribution.

When I first asked Lani what specific suggestions she had for others she laughingly replied, "Oh, that's a toughie. I was hoping you'd find the

answer for that!" But almost immediately she specified a list that emphasized the personal qualities and competencies of the *ho'oponopono*
leader.

> O.K. For those who want to use it my feelings are they have to have skills.
> Good helping skills of relating, of communicating. To me that's basic.
> They've got to be able to display the kind of personality that puts forth a
> sense of security, and of trust, and in command. Yet warmth. Yet a firmness
> that's going to demand from the group, "I want work." That it's not an easy
> thing. . . . Commitment of the person. Also to do their own studying about
> beliefs and practices, above and beyond what one might get from learning
> *ho'oponopono.* That to me would be critical because the families might
> come up with some other areas of spiritualism. And no matter how you
> view the subject, it's the client's belief system. And that you've gotta' deal
> with, you've gotta' weave in.
>
> So it's not only being sure of oneself and your abilities to do, or to be
> helpful. And not only to get the training to use and understanding the
> method of *ho'oponopono,* but also going beyond that—where the process
> becomes a motivating factor for you to set up challenges so that you can
> build upon what's already started. And if they can get to that point where
> they're saying, "I've done it with a family. I wonder if I can do it with a
> group of nonrelated people?"—that's the kind of enthusiasm, that's the kind
> of openness I'd like. "You know, I didn't do this so well. And I'm not certain.
> And I wanna' find out about it. Can you sit down and have a discussion
> about it?" The openness to discuss. To look at alternative ways. The willing-
> ness to risk! And say, "Gee. I don't know too much about that. Maybe you
> can tell me about it." Being able to do that because it rises from a surety, a
> confidence about oneself.
>
> I also recognize that more knowledge, flexible attitudes, and refined skills
> come with experience. I wasn't like this when I first started. When I started I
> said, "Only with Hawaiians. Only with families and with a Hawaiian
> worker." And at this point I'm saying, "Baloney." It's not limited to that! But
> I couldn't say that then. But now I can. I can feel it and operate it.

SUMMARY

The accounts of the eight individuals interviewed represent a variety of
contemporary uses and styles of *ho'oponopono,* although all stemmed
from the single form described by Pukui. The contexts of use differed
widely from the most traditional—use by a Hawaiian leader with a
Hawaiian family—to entirely new situations—use by non-Hawaiian
leaders with non-Hawaiian groups of unrelated people. Diverse backgrounds in terms of ethnicity, education, and training may have accounted for some of the different interpretations.

Because all the individuals learned about the practice from the same general source, I believe that despite the variations they would recognize the other forms and styles. It remains as the major work in chapter 4 to take a closer look at the collection of interviews and to discern areas of agreement and disagreement. The purpose of this comparison is not to illustrate a right or wrong form of ho'oponopono but to clarify what ho'oponopono is. Is it possible to cull out the essential elements of the practice from other elements? Is what individuals say they are doing really ho'oponopono, or is it a new problem-solving method that weaves some ho'oponopono conventions with other group methods? These are some of the questions to consider in the final chapters.

CHAPTER 3 NOTES

1. I owe a debt of gratitude to the following authors whose concrete methodological suggestions were very instructive: Lofland (1971, 1976), Bogdan and Taylor (1975), and Spradley and McCurdy (1972).

2. The person who declined to take part in the study said he objected to the premise of "adaptation" that was implied in the research. He believed that being part of the study might be seen by others as a tacit sanction of the various ho'oponopono uses described in the interviews. He had many reservations about the variations because he thought they might not do justice to the form and essence of traditional ho'oponopono.

3. The value of intensive or unstructured interviewing in descriptive studies of social interaction has been outlined by Lofland (1971, 1976), Bogdan and Taylor (1975), and Spradley and McCurdy (1972) based on the field research of sociologists and anthropologists. Some of the benefits of this interviewing method include the researcher's enhanced opportunity to: (1) engage in face-to-face interaction, which is the most comprehensive way to know another person or situation; (2) gain a perspective from the subject's point of view and receive information in the subject's own terms; (3) explore concepts in great detail; (4) examine the contradictions and paradoxes that are a part of a person's experience; and (5) assign human meaning to a situation that could provide the context and background for later statistical studies of a more general nature. The main limitation of this type of interviewing is that the interviewer needs to be cautious about drawing conclusions about behavior or activities solely from what people say about those occurrences. Ideally it is desirable to check the consistency of reporting of occurrences by carrying out unobtrusive observations, if possible. The only time I was able to do this in my study was in the drug abuse program. In this case I found the descriptions by Virginia Wahler and Robert Padua to be generally consistent with my observations. This also included their conclusions that the boys in the program were enthusiastic about their daily ho'oponopono sessions. The most extraordinary evidence of this enthusiasm was one boy's new arm tattoo that said "Ho'oponopono."

4. A rationale for this type of pre-interview work is provided by Hunt, Crane, and Wahlke (1964), who concluded that interviewers need to be intelligent and well informed about the interview topic prior to the interview. Pareek and Venka-

teswara Rao (1980) wrote about "authenticity" of responses in interviews and found that the likelihood of effective cross-cultural interviews is greatly enhanced when the interviewer is well acquainted with the interview topics.

5. Names of others who have used *ho'oponopono* were given to me, but after consultation with both Hawaiian and academic advisers, I decided that a sample of eight was sufficient in number and representativeness.

6. Obtaining research categories in this manner is recommended by Glaser and Strauss (1967) in their work discussing the use of "grounded theory" building in the social sciences.

7. A relationship seems to exist between having an advanced degree and the tendency toward being cosmopolitan or nonprovincial. Rogers and Shoemaker (1971, 108, 189) have pointed out that cosmopolitan individuals are more likely to be both aware of innovations and prone to adopt innovations earlier than others.

8. The two are also the individuals whose model of *ho'oponopono* appears in chapter 4.

9. Because of the relatively small network of people familiar with social services on Oahu, it is possible that some in this group will recognize the individuals or agencies involved in this study. All participants in the study were aware of this possibility and had no serious objections to it.

CHAPTER 4

Variations in Hoʻoponopono

The preceding chapter gave a general overview of *hoʻoponopono* use and the attitudes toward it by eight individuals who were interviewed for this study. In chapter 4 the twofold purpose is: (1) to examine some of the ways these individuals varied their actual practice of *hoʻoponopono*, and (2) to outline a complete model of *hoʻoponopono* that has been used by two individuals who have extensive experience with the process.

Before proceeding with this examination it is helpful to review a few things. First, the nature of this work is to describe how *hoʻoponopono* has been adapted, adaptation implying degrees of variability. Each of the case study examples departed in some way from the traditional pattern. Second, because each individual had a unique experience with the process, the different opinions and circumstances about the modifications will be cited. The opinions or comments covered topics such as the purpose of *hoʻoponopono*, how the individual learned about it, his or her assessment of the practice, barriers to its use, and suggestions or recommendations for others to consider.

EXAMINING THE AREAS OF
AGREEMENT AND DISAGREEMENT

The variations will be categorized under four headings that correspond to the general sequence of steps in *hoʻoponopono:* (1) opening phase, which includes assessment and preparation of participants through the formal statement of the problem; (2) discussion phase, which includes all discussions that lead toward identification of the problem and the ensuing ramifications; (3) resolution phase, when confession, forgiveness, and release occur and restitution is set if necessary; and (4) closing phase, which includes the summary and closing ritual.

Opening Phase

The four topics concerning the opening phase are client preparation, assessment, use of terms, and opening ritual. Through analysis of the collected case studies, I concluded that client preparation varied both in amount and method. The division seemed to coincide with the occupation of the leaders. The three social workers—Keola, Kalau, and Lani—all elaborated on the importance of doing a lot of preparation before beginning *hoʻoponopono*. Kalau in particular stressed the need for developing a trusting relationship with the family involved. Next, the steps of *hoʻoponopono* were explained and necessary agreements were made. Once this was done *hoʻoponopono* began. Both Lani and Kalau said they continued to remind the participants about the events of each stage of *hoʻoponopono* until they were thoroughly familiar with it. The other leaders from the drug treatment and wilderness programs did not prepare in quite the same way. The participants in these programs were already involved in many activities designed to build and enhance relationships. *Hoʻoponopono* was only one of these activities. All leaders stressed teaching the groups about *hoʻoponopono* before using it. The wilderness course instructors explained the process on the second day of the course and let the students know it was available to them if needed. Robert, from the drug program, said that the boys were formally taught the process, but more importantly, they learned through the experience of using it on a daily basis.

Part of the preparation phase involved assembling a group to determine whether the use of *hoʻoponopono* would be beneficial. Again, the variations divided along occupational lines. For the three social workers this assessment was an important part of their work since the relationship with clients was voluntary; for the others, use of *hoʻoponopono* was a regular part of their programs. If a person signed up for the drug abuse or wilderness program, they were involved in *hoʻoponopono*. However, all leaders in this group made a distinction between *hoʻoponopono* attendance, which was mandatory, and personal sharing, which was voluntary.

One of the issues on which I tried to gather information during the interviews was whether a leader believed that certain values were prerequisites to *hoʻoponopono* use. In other words, did the leader assess the group to determine whether certain values were held by the group members as a precondition to using *hoʻoponopono*? As the interview proceeded I began to realize that it was difficult to distinguish between prerequisite values in participants and implicit values in the process. Some of the values I investigated were interdependence, concern for the group, ability to express feelings, truthfulness, sincerity, patience, belief in retribution, spirituality, high group trust, and importance of ethnocultural commonalities. Most individuals in the study affirmed that these qualities were sometimes present before the sessions and seemed to develop further during the sessions, but there was no agreement about whether any one value or cluster of values was particularly crucial. As part of the preparation, all the individuals mentioned ground rules such as self-scrutiny, truthfulness, and sincerity specified in *Nānā I Ke Kumu* (Pukui et al. 1972, 62). But I found no example of a leader halting the process because a particular value was lacking in the group. I still have a sense that the issue of value congruence between client and method is an important one, and if in the future individuals explore the use of *ho'oponopono* with other cultural groups, then preassessment may be crucial.

During the preparation phase each leader had to decide whether to use the Hawaiian terms to explain the process. The usage choice varied among the leaders. The wilderness program leaders—Jean, Joseph, and Paul—used the formal Hawaiian terms, a practice that fit with the program's goal of teaching the students pertinent Hawaiian cultural facts. However, Joseph used English terms when he conducted *ho'oponopono* sessions on the mainland. Other individuals in the study varied the use of terms according to the situation. While teaching the process to the boys in the drug treatment program, Virginia and Robert used the formal terms, but in the daily sessions they often substituted English equivalents. However, they persisted in using the term *pule,* which they believed was more acceptable to the boys than using the term "prayer." It seemed that Keola, Kalau, and Lani used the Hawaiian terms if they were working with more traditional Hawaiian people and used English terms with other people.

The traditional formal opening and closing of *ho'oponopono* included a *pule* to the Hawaiian spiritual forces or to the Christian God, or to both. The adaptation of this spiritual element to the various settings in this study was a somewhat sensitive issue. In most cases the opening *pule* was at least a time for setting a serious tone for the work to follow. The three social workers sometimes used the phrase "powers that be" in place of references to specific deities. Virginia also felt comfortable with that phrase and described the *pule* as "pulling in the strength of the source." For Robert, *pule* was "asking for spiritual strength." The drug treatment program was federally funded, thereby restricting Virginia and Robert from making specific denominational references. The term *pule* was used in the wilderness school, but the form was individualized. Jean said her *pule* was usually addressed to the "universal spirits, or to the people in the group and the *aloha* that is in the energy here." For Joseph the prayer was a built-in part of the process; he sometimes invoked "gods or spirits." At other times he did a sensory awareness or relaxation narrative. Paul said his prayer usually asked "for some strength and commitment and guidance—and affirming the place we're in."

The closing *pule* was distinguished from the opening *pule* by most of the leaders. For Lani and Paul, the closing ritual was a summary of what had taken place and a reaffirmation of positive group relations. Virginia, Jean, and Joseph made specific reference to *pule* as a statement of thanks. Kalau and Keola did not specify details about the closing *pule* in their sessions.

Not all leaders agreed on the centrality of the spiritual focus to *hoʻoponopono*. Virginia and Robert emphasized spirituality as being the key ingredient of the process. Robert said, "The basis is the spirit—that's the key to making it work." Paul believed similarly, explaining, "I think the power of *hoʻoponopono* lies in the spiritual qualities it embraces." Because of this attitude Paul found it difficult to translate the spiritual quality for use in a secular mediation setting. Keola stated that the spiritual belief of a participant plays a central role because "it lends dignity to the process," and he reminded participants that "the implications are much greater than you and I can understand." Lani mentioned "belief in something" as important for participants but did not stress it as strongly as some of the others. Kalau did not think that the spiritual value of *hoʻoponopono* posed a difficulty. "Well, in today's world where so many people are kind of putting religion back into their lives, I don't know that that would be such big a problem." Jean emphasized the spiritual aspects of *hoʻoponopono* more from a historical perspective. Joseph used the *pule* and thought spirituality was an important factor for the *haku* but did not think it was essential for the others. He said, "I don't suppose you have to have these spiritual beliefs for it to work as a psychotherapy."[1]

Discussion Phase

The role of *haku* was fairly consistent for most individuals in the case studies. The leader facilitated the process, identified the problem area, listened to the others, clarified the discussion, and generally maintained a controlled and safe atmosphere that encouraged honest and sincere expressions by the participants. One of the other ground rules stated in *Nānā I Ke Kumu* was that the *haku* was someone who was not involved in the *hihia*. This allowed the *haku* to be impartial and open-minded during the process. However, one of the individuals, Lani, told of two sessions she led when she also was a central part of the problem. When I asked if she had felt any conflict in the role, she replied, "No. My sense as a helper overrode that."

Another departure from the traditional leadership role was shared by Lani and Keola. When they have worked with a family for a period of time, they try to sense the family's readiness to assume a leadership role.

If a husband or wife seems ready, then Lani and Keola begin to play a less active part. Keola said, "In that process we're there more as resource persons. A lot of times we're there just to help them check out whether they're on the right track or not." Eventually this leads to ending their involvement completely. Lani and Keola were the only persons interviewed who had used this variation.

Nānā I Ke Kumu (1972) also stated that the *haku* had the responsibility of channeling all the discussion. All group members spoke directly to the leader, who could then ask for clarification or could relay a concern or message to another group member. This method contrasts with most Western therapies, which encourage individuals to speak directly to one another.

A range of deviation from the practice of channeling all discussion was evident among the individuals interviewed. Two of the individuals, Virginia and Kalau, seemed to follow the original guideline. Kalau specified that talking only to the leader was a rule that the family had to agree to follow. "Those rules, I think, are very important. Especially the one where there's communication only through the leader." She reasoned that this kept a lid on angry emotions and allowed the participants to communicate more effectively.

Lani and Keola basically adhered to the guideline and traditional reasoning but made an exception at one stage of the process. During the *mihi, kala,* and *oki* when positive signs of forgiveness, caring, and love were apt to be expressed, Lani and Keola allow participants to speak to one another directly. Keola said he believed this modification "lends to the process." This also coincides with what Lani saw as the role of the *haku*—"to prevent further *hihia* from occurring and to become the facilitator for these positive elements to move through."

The remaining four individuals preferred to encourage the participants to talk directly to each other. Talking through the leader was enforced only when the communication became blocked. Joseph leaned more toward the control and channeling part of the continuum. Robert preferred an informal discussion with the group. Paul tried to get participants to talk to one another and only mediated if the situation got out of hand. Jean agreed with Paul's view and saw the *haku* more as one who regulated the flow of conversation.

When tempers flared or interruptions occurred in the discussion phase, *Nānā I Ke Kumu* (1972) specified that a *ho'omalu* should be called. This is known as a cooling-off period, a time for reflection on what has just happened and a chance to be reminded of the essential purpose of problem solving. All the individuals interviewed admitted that they had used this strategy, although they had different guidelines about when it should be used. The policy differences seemed related to the person's view of how anger should be handled. The traditional Hawaiian view was that the expression of negative emotions, such as anger, did not serve a useful purpose; it only created further *hihia* and compounded the problem. This style contrasts with some schools of therapy and counseling where the expression of anger is seen as potentially having a positive, freeing, cathartic effect. Most Western therapeutic practices are oriented toward relieving an individual's suffering; *hoʻoponopono* focuses more on the relief of tensions in the relationships among group members.

One leader who preferred to allow the anger to surface rather than to call a *hoʻomalu* realized that this was not usual *hoʻoponopono* procedure and asked not to be quoted. (On this one issue I will not identify by name any of the viewpoints, which will ensure the confidentiality requested by this individual.)

Another person had a similar view and believed that interruptions and other outbursts could uncover problems more directly. A philosophy expressed by another individual espoused the positive value in allowing individuals to both verbally express and physically act out angry feelings. However, within the context of a *hoʻoponopono* session, the leader would most likely call a *hoʻomalu* if angry behavior occurred. During the *hoʻomalu*, the leader might take the angry person aside and help him or her release the anger in a physical way to avoid harming himself or others. Tension-releasing exercises, strenuous physical activities, and other creative alternatives were mentioned as ways of ventilating angry feelings. Once accomplished, the person could rejoin the group and talk about his or her feelings in a calmer fashion. The other leaders interviewed did not say much about ways to respond to disruptive behaviors. A few emphasized the importance of maintaining control of communication so that negative comments or behaviors were generally not allowed.

A final issue about the role of the leader emerged during the interviews and involved the amount and kind of questioning the leader pursued during the sessions. *Nānā I Ke Kumu* emphasized participant self-scrutinization of "conduct, attitudes, and emotions" (Pukui et al. 1972, 62). Yet certainly in *hoʻoponopono* sessions that involved complex problems, the degree of resolution would be related to the degree of depth and thoroughness that the leader was able to encourage during the discussions.

Not all individuals made direct comments about detailed questions. Three people said that they thought in-depth questioning or probing was part of the leader's responsibility. Three others were hesitant and gave more conditional responses. It is possible that the amount of questioning each person did, in practice, may not have varied much from the others. If I used the word "probing" as a synonym for "questioning" in the interview, some people shied away from an affirmative response, possibly because the word "probing" had a negative, intrusive connotation.

Three individuals indicated that they did a lot of questioning. I asked Paul, "How much questioning do you do?" and he replied, "Oh, a lot of probing and clarifying questions." Lani was asked about "questioning or probing" and she said she allowed participants to share whatever they were ready to share. She added, however, "If I feel that they're not giving me the kind of depth that's required, my task is to initiate those questions and to get the response from them." She said she checked out their feelings to determine whether or not they were unduly uncomfortable. Her tactics included alternating deep questioning and surface questioning, returning to deeper questions when the person was more comfortable. Lani used the term *wehe wehe* to distinguish superficial discussions from therapeutic discussions that get more to the core of things. When I asked Keola about his questioning or probing he answered, "The leader does a lot. As a matter of fact the leader does a lot of clarification, asking more specific questions." Keola believed that asking questions of one person compelled other group members to examine themselves also. He thought the leader's questions were particularly helpful when a person was feeling stuck.

In contrast, Robert cautioned about questioning individuals or digging deeper. "That's a very delicate situation. I use my own judgment if I'm going to cut into it." He sensed that the boys he worked with were "battered up inside," so he asked for "spiritual strength and guidance" to determine the extent of his questioning. Robert said that most of the time he did not probe and let the boys say whatever they wanted on their own. Virginia worked with the same boys and pretty much agreed with Robert about "questioning and probing." Virginia tried to emphasize to the boys that they could all be leaders, that they did not need a lot of "counseling-type skills and insights." As she said, "Simply follow the process. The process heals, so we don't probe." The one exception occurred early in the course when the boys were still learning the process and forming relationships. At this stage, when some of the boys picked on another who was not able to adequately speak for himself, Virginia protected that boy by questioning the others for him. In summing up this topic though, Virginia returned the focus to the need for each boy to assume responsibility for himself. "A boy must know that to receive, he must ask. And he must trust the process."

Resolution Phase

The resolution stage of the *ho'oponopono* process did not always take place, according to some leaders. Although traditionally there was always the possibility that a group would be unwilling or unable to proceed to the resolution phase, if this occurred it was a grave matter with serious consequences. The individual or individuals were said to be *ho'omauhala* (holding on to the problem; holding a grudge). Failure to forgive could precipitate repercussions from the spiritual world and from the group members through ostracization, or *mo ka piko*. The belief in this kind of retribution is not as strong today. The individual's allegiance to the group is not as binding either, which may account for a greater acceptance of deleting the resolution phase. Some leaders mentioned holding *ho'oponopono* sessions without an expectation of problem resolution; two quite different examples of this were presented in the interviews. Virginia mentioned one example of using *ho'oponopono* as a preventive session—a forum for the boys to come together at the end of the day to share how things were going. If during the opening discussion no problems emerged, everyone shared whatever they chose and the process ended with a *pule*. The other example was given by Lani and Keola, who both had come to the conclusion that using *ho'oponopono* as a diagnostic or assessment tool was in itself very worthwhile and complete. They thought it was most helpful when the group moved through the forgiveness stage so that harmony could be restored, but if that was not possible, then thoroughly identifying the problem was sufficient. After thorough discussion, they proceeded to the closing phase.

The complete resolution phase includes the procedure for the confession, forgiveness, and release. In the past the *haku* played a central part in the *mihi, kala,* and *oki* by mediating the articulated apologies. The *haku*'s role has become less crucial in this area, as was discussed in the previous section. At least six of the leaders—Lani, Keola, Joseph, Paul, Jean, and Robert—preferred the group members to speak directly with one another during this phase. Sometimes the *mihi, kala,* and *oki* were specific and articulated: the act of transgression was named and the apology and forgiveness were stated. In other cases the process was more nonverbal. Robert said that the boys displayed forgiveness in a "natural" way. "They stand up, grab each other, drop some tears, laugh." Lani and Keola also looked for various nonverbal cues such as hugging, caring looks, and kissing as signs that the resolution had been sincere and deep.

Closing Phase

All *ho'oponopono* sessions had some type of closing statement or ritual. The specific form and content varied, but all leaders included a *pule*. This was usually a prayer of thanks or appreciation and sometimes included a summary of what had happened. In addition to the *pule* or sometimes within it, additional remarks were made. Kalau said that this could be a time for a family to make plans for the future. Jean used this time to remind the group that the problems resolved were now *pau*; a *ho'omalu* was put on them so they would not be discussed further. Lani made a distinction in the use of this kind of *ho'omalu*. The family or group was free to discuss the matter as long as they did not get into a discussion that could create further *hihia.*

In these cases, the *pani,* or sharing of a snack or meal after a session, was not always done. Playing, swimming, or a period of quiet time were often substituted in the wilderness courses. But according to Keola the *pani* was the actual closure of the process. He gave his view on the symbolic importance of food during the closing phase: "Food is important. And in food, when your natural juices are moving, one tends to be much more in the mood to share in fellowship, able to relax. When you have a full stomach, one feels a lot better. So I think it lends to the process."

A SOCIAL WORK MODEL OF HO‘OPONOPONO

The model of *ho‘oponopono* presented here is an outline of the process used by Lani and Keola Espiritu. It is a form of *ho‘oponopono* that synthesizes the traditional process taught by Mary Kawena Pukui and skills and insight from the social work field. As part-Hawaiians, both Lani and Keola believe that their personal experiences involving Hawaiian values and practices have enhanced their understanding of *ho‘oponopono.* Although they strongly identified themselves as Hawaiians, they also perceived *ho‘oponopono* as a process that had applicability to other groups. Earlier Keola was quoted as saying, "It makes good mental health practice."

I chose to present their model of *ho‘oponopono* rather than another model for three reasons. First, of the eight people I interviewed, Lani and Keola have the most experience using the practice, both in number of years and in variety of contexts. Second, because they are social workers, their particular conceptual framework may be the most useful to other family or group counselors. Finally, the model can be used to analyze the example of the *ho‘oponopono* session in chapter 1 since Lani and Keola appeared there as parents of the Kealoha family.

Although the general model is credited to both Lani and Keola, Lani alone worked with me to formulate the outline. As an additional aid to the reader, figure 1 presents a simplified flow chart that shows how the process generally proceeds and includes "feedback loops" that represent alternative paths in the process.

The model describes four phases of using *ho‘oponopono* with families or groups. These are the same phases—opening, discussion, resolution, and closing—that were used in the previous section. The chart gives the Hawaiian terms for the steps and a brief conceptual equivalent for each. Two important points that were presented in chapter 3 may bear reiteration. The first is that Lani and Keola articulated three purposes or uses of *ho‘oponopono:* problem assessment or diagnosis, correction or remedia-

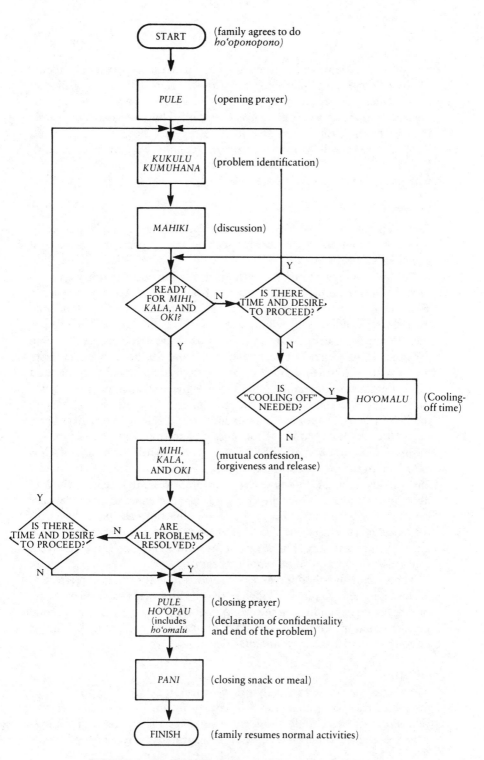

FIGURE 1. Simplified Flow Chart of *Ho'oponopono* Session

tion of the problem, and prevention of problem escalation. The outcome of any of these, particularly the corrective or remedial, can be either an enhancement of group functioning and cohesiveness or a decision to sever a relationship in the group, as exemplified by a decision by a couple to separate or divorce. The second issue repeated here is that Lani and Keola have expanded their use of *ho'oponopono* beyond working with Hawaiian families. This model has been used with non-Hawaiians and with groups of unrelated people.

Opening Phase

The beginning of the process includes preparing the group for participation in *ho'oponopono,* the opening statement or prayer, and the general statement of the problem.

Ideally the preparation time with the group includes making an assessment about the family's or group's beliefs and values. Lani specified five areas she examines: (1) the extent of belief in retribution, which may be related to the individual's willingness to forgive and release; (2) whether there is a positive attitude toward change as a part of the problem-solving process; (3) the degree of understanding of how conflict creates entanglements with others; (4) the degree to which participants understand and can maintain confidentiality; and (5) the degree to which the group holds the values of cooperation, trust, and interconnectedness, which are implicit in *ho'oponopono.* Lani's examination of these issues gives her a better idea of further instruction and preparation required before she begins *ho'oponopono* with the family or group. When the process itself is described to the group Lani fully explains each concept and its rationale. She also explains the consequences of not following the steps and procedures of the process. Once the group has been oriented the members are asked if they wish to proceed. If there are objections the procedure calls for *kūkulu kumuhana* (individual counseling) with the objecting individuals. The process may stop at this point if the resistance is not resolved; otherwise, the formal *ho'oponopono* begins.

The *pule* or opening prayer sets a serious tone for the group effort to follow. Lani and Keola use "powers that be" in their prayer or may use other phrases depending on the group's beliefs and practices. The general problem that precipitated the *ho'oponopono* is then stated. This is another form of *kūkulu kumuhana.*

Discussion Phase

The discussion phase is usually the most lengthy since it involves all the discussions necessary to uncover the core problem. The term for this process is *mahiki,* which refers to identifying and working through one specific aspect at a time. *Mahiki* may be repeated many times when the problem has many complex layers. Each time the *mahiki* is done it should lead to a clear identification of an initial transgression, or *hala*. The negative repercussions that were felt in the group's network of relationships, as a result of the *hala*, should also be identified and discussed at this time. The entangling web of adverse effects is the *hihia*. Each *hihia* has to be untangled by going through the resolution phase of forgiveness, release, and severance before discussion begins on another *hihia*. During the discussion the participants and the leader have distinct roles. The participants are expected to engage in self-scrutiny to clearly discern their part in the problem. The emphasis is on honesty and the expression of one's own feelings and perspectives. Open communication, which includes good listening and self-expression, is encouraged. The leader generally controls the flow of communication and channels most of the discussion. Lani uses the term *wehe wehe* to describe the kind of in-depth questioning that the leader pursues to uncover and clarify the issues in the problem.

Another important responsibility of the leader is to constantly monitor the verbal and nonverbal communication of the participants. This means that the leader focuses not only on the content of what happened in the past but also on the process of interaction in the present. The goal is to nurture a sense of mutual understanding of the problem, both cognitively and emotionally. The leader also provides safeguards for the group by preventing emotional outbursts and channeling the discussion. If tempers flare or other strong emotions surface, a *ho'omalu*, or reflective cooling-off period, is called. Participants then are directed to consider what prompted the emotions and encouraged to regain their sense of purpose and goodwill.

Once the discussion has led to a clear understanding of each *hihia* and *hala*, the leader asks if the group is ready to move on to a solution. If any individual is not ready, the leader has a number of alternatives. A *ho'omalu* can be called on that particular problem until the individual has worked through whatever resistance he or she has. In the meantime, the other group members can go on to another layer of the problem. Unwillingness to forgive can also indicate that the problem has not been discussed or articulated clearly enough. The procedure in this situation is to return to *kūkulu kumuhana* (as problem identification) and *mahiki*. *Kūkulu kumuhana* can also mean working with a person individually to overcome the resistance. In some situations the group may come to an impasse, making resolution unlikely or impossible. The *ho'oponopono* may have to proceed directly to the closing phase with a summary of what had been diagnosed as the problem and entanglements. In this situation, *ho'oponopono* has been successful only to the extent of assessing and identifying the problem situation. *Mo ka piko*, or severing a relationship due to the inability of a person to forgive, is also a possibility when a group or person has failed to come to resolution. However, in most cases these alternatives are unnecessary and the group agrees to proceed.

Resolution Phase

Resolution in *ho'oponopono* includes mutual requests for forgiveness and release and severance of all the hurt associated with the problem. Restitution may also be discussed and set, then the problem is declared closed pending payment of the restitution.

The *mihi, kala,* and *oki* is a multi-step process that occurs between each pair of participants involved in each *hihia*. Each person must separately admit his or her wrongdoing and be forgiven by the other involved. After each person has done this, the group members can mutually release and cut off the negative entanglements that have bound them together. Figure 2 illustrates how this transaction takes place.

Lani and Keola allow the individuals to communicate directly with each other during the resolution phase. However, the leader still checks each step for indications of genuine expression by each person. One way to do this is to look for congruence in the verbal and nonverbal messages communicated.

If during the earlier discussion the need for restitution was mentioned then the group has to decide what the nature of the reparations will be. In some instances the final resolution of the problem is not considered complete until restitution has been made. Once arrangements for restitution have been made and the *mihi, kala,* and *oki* have occurred, the leader declares the problem closed. This final *ho'omalu* includes instructions to the group to avoid any further discussion of the problem that might create negative repercussions. However, positive, affirming discussion within the group is allowed after the session.

If the group has other problems to be resolved then the process returns to the *kūkulu kumuhana* and *mahiki.* If it is time for the particular session to close, or if the whole treatment process is finished, then the group proceeds to the closing steps.

Closing Phase

The general structure of the closing part is the same whether it closes a session or a series of sessions in a treatment process. The content of the summary and closing ritual reflects what has occurred and reaffirms the group's bonds and shared experiences.

The *pule ho'opau,* or closing prayer, is primarily one of thanks and includes a summary of what has been resolved and accomplished and an affirmation of the positive individual or group functioning. Statements

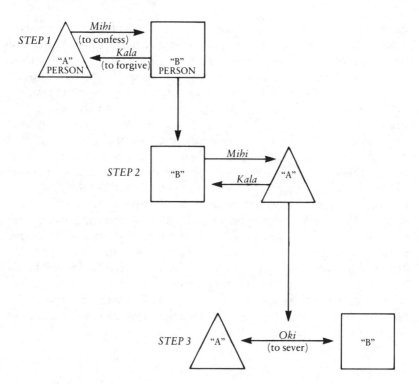

FIGURE 2. Transactions during the Resolution Phase

may be made to indicate problem areas on which the group will work in the future.

The *pani* formally closes the problem-solving sessions. At this time the leader and group members share a snack or meal together. Lani believes that the leader should also contribute part of the snack. This is a transition time for the group to reenter more normal patterns of interaction, to relax and enjoy one another.

SUMMARY

The individuals in the case studies shared some areas of agreement in attitudes. But rather than analyze the degree of similarity, I allowed the subtle differences to remain as a way to hold the portrait of the person's experience intact.[2] However, during the course of the study, areas of differentiation rather consistently stood out. Further analysis of these areas can be fruitful and reveal clues about the future evolution of *ho'opono-pono*. These differences are also the ones that beg further clarification and discussion, perhaps among the current practitioners of *ho'opono-pono*. If *ho'oponopono* is to remain a practice that has recognizable traits, then there will need to be a minimum consistency in the practice. When a significant segment of the society agrees that a particular config-uration of traits constitutes the practice of *ho'oponopono*, it may increase the likelihood of its continued use. But if the future trend is toward further individualization, then the resulting divergence will destroy the impact of *ho'oponopono* as a problem-solving process rooted in the Hawaiian cultural experience. Another consideration is that the interactive nature of any therapeutic process accounts for a degree of var-iability. The interaction comprises at least three operating factors: the therapist (including style and skill), the problem (including situation and setting), and the client (including personality and attitudes). There is a certain dilemma in trying to ascertain which variations described by the individuals are due to situational factors and which are actually serious departures from the essence of *ho'oponopono* as a specific, recognizable cultural phenomenon. I believe the variations described are on the cut-ting edge of this issue and are further explored in chapter 5.

CHAPTER 4 NOTES

1. Other evidence shows that the spiritual tone of *ho'oponopono* may be a controversial issue. In an article about *ho'oponopono* use in a public high school on the island of Maui, Nishihara (1978) said he omitted the *pule* and spiritual references altogether. I also spoke with a social worker who was contemplating using *ho'oponopono* but had not yet reconciled with himself how he would do the *pule,* or deal with the spiritual element. Coming to terms with this element would require self-scrutiny and clarification of his own spiritual beliefs and expression of them. He would also have to find a way to assess a family's spiritual beliefs and practices. The spiritual issue could be a barrier for individuals who have the necessary knowledge and skills to use *ho'oponopono*.

2. In descriptive studies there is value in letting an individual's words stand alone and in context without a great deal of distillation or generalization. Again, Cottle (1977) is a resource for this perspective.

CHAPTER 5

Conclusions and Implications

The transfer of a non-Western, indigenous problem-solving process to more multicultural contexts is a novel occurrence. The first examination of such an occurrence is like traversing new territory—there are no reliable maps to guide the way, making it difficult to know if you have even been able to survey the boundaries. I hope this presentation has provided an initial survey of a new territory in cross-cultural mental health. Like newly discovered or rediscovered territory, it needs further exploration to truly appreciate the riches and lessons that may lie therein. So while this study posits some conclusions, which follow, it also raises further questions and thoughts for others to consider.

THE LEADERS INVOLVED

Background Similarities

The discovery that most of the eight persons interviewed had similar training and education was an unexpected one. I chose the term "human relations" to classify the commonality. This finding, which was presented in chapter 3, might be explained as coincidental because of the small sample, or it might indicate that a particular type of human relations value or skill orientation within the mental health field complements *ho'oponopono*. It might also suggest that the skills developed in human relations training provide a basis for the use of *ho'oponopono*.

Training

Since most individuals in the study seemed to have similar orientations, both in training and education, the question arises: Are these orientations actually prerequisites to the contemporary use of *ho'oponopono*?

The question is especially pertinent to individuals who did not grow up with an emphasis on traditional Hawaiian values; such a group is likely to include most prospective *ho'oponopono* leaders. More to the point, is the leader required to have a particular personal value orientation in order to lead *ho'oponopono*? And what degree of training, skills, and competencies might be necessary?

Two Initial Approaches to Using Ho'oponopono

The leaders began using *ho'oponopono* in either of two ways: starting with parts of it and adding more as they felt comfortable doing so, or adopting the whole system at once. Although in the former situation it could be concluded that the leader was not really using *ho'oponopono* until most of the parts were included, this component approach may suggest a way for others to learn to use *ho'oponopono*. If a person did not feel comfortable using the complete process at once, the partial approach could encourage a thorough understanding of each component of the process initially. This approach might also involve fewer risks than adopting the complete process at one time.

Audiences

The eight leaders did not agree on who constituted an appropriate audience for *ho'oponopono* use. Some leaders' views changed with time; they initially worked only with families but later worked with groups of unrelated individuals. Many other considerations were mentioned. Some thought *ho'oponopono*'s use should be limited to "local" or island residents while others thought it had a broader appeal. A few thought it was inappropriate for groups who had businesslike relationships, while others had used it in precisely that situation. Two people successfully used *ho'oponopono* with a man who was known to have psychiatric problems, yet another person believed this practice was not advisable. Some strived to make sure that the group had certain values and beliefs before proceeding while for others this was unnecessary. Clearly there was no agreement on the matter of audience, and it is difficult to determine the basis for each leader's reasons. For some, experience, personal style, or preference may have prompted the stance, while for others personal feelings or conjectures about audience suitability may have influenced their opinions.

Transfer-to-Client System

A few leaders mentioned that after working with a group for a period of time, sometimes group members not only learned the practice of *ho'oponopono* for themselves but were also able to apply it in a different setting on their own. In all cases this was a spontaneous occurrence that both surprised and pleased the original leaders. Is it possible that with more deliberate effort this transference of *ho'oponopono* to the client could become a realistic outcome of working with a group or family? A more in-depth study of spontaneous transference cases might yield a set of factors that could be duplicated with other groups to increase the transference likelihood.

THE CONTEXT OF THE PROCESS

Ho'oponopono as an Alternative Mental Health Strategy

As pointed out earlier, the contemporary uses of *ho'oponopono* can be related to the recent trend in developing alternative mental health services, particularly ones that have specific cultural relevance. The reemergence of *ho'oponopono* was due largely to the work of the Queen Liliuokalani Children's Center. The subsequent publication and popularity of the first volume of *Nānā I Ke Kumu* suggested that there was local interest in providing such alternatives for Hawaiian people. Paglinawan's 1972 study concluded that social workers could use *ho'oponopono* with Hawaiian families. Her efforts later led to the production of videotapes on the subject to be used for training family workers.[1] What is unique about the use of *ho'oponopono* as presented in my study is that the majority of the leaders interviewed were using the process in a totally innovative context—with non-Hawaiians, with groups of people who were not related, and sometimes with leaders who were not Hawaiians. The innovation leads me to conclude that there is something in *ho'oponopono* that has a transcultural appeal. Some of the features named as having special attraction, in addition to the obvious cultural specificity of terms and concepts, included the high degree of explicitness in procedures and roles, the inclusion of forgiveness and release, the spiritual element, the conceptualization of relationship entanglements that proceed from problems, and the high degree of control and risk management that the process afforded both the leader and participants.

Ho'oponopono within a Program Setting

Almost all the leaders had used *ho'oponopono* within a program or agency setting that had a strong commitment to recognizing and reinforcing local cultural traditions. Two programs, the wilderness school and the residential drug abuse treatment program, integrated cultural experiences, values, and practices into their curricula. *Ho'oponopono* was just one of many features of the two programs that emphasized Hawaiian culture. This integration may indicate that agencies or programs that have already made commitments to the inclusion of cultural components

might be more likely to adopt *ho'oponopono* or other culture-based strategies. Training and support opportunities would probably enhance this
possibility, as was suggested in some of the interviews.

Case Follow-Up

Determining therapeutic efficacy is a difficult and controversial task. In
the case of *ho'oponopono* use, no longitudinal study has been conducted
to formally follow-up with groups or families that used *ho'oponopono* to
see if positive changes were maintained. It would be interesting to design
a controlled study where fairly similar case outcomes were compared:
cases that used *ho'oponopono,* cases treated with conventional family
therapy, and untreated cases. Although such studies are time consuming,
complex, and expensive, it seems a worthwhile area for research, an area
that will be particularly necessary if non-Western therapy approaches are
to ever compare with Western approaches and gain a degree of recognition, acceptance, and use.

THE MEANING AND FUTURE OF HO'OPONOPONO

Possible Variations

Chapter 4 elaborated on the *ho'oponopono* steps that showed the most
variation. It seems that the features of *ho'oponopono* most distinctively
Hawaiian are the ones subject to change, either through deletion or
adaptation. One example is the use of the *pule.* Generally, counseling
and therapy in the United States are secular enterprises and do not
include specific spiritual practices. However, since current trends toward
holistic mental health approaches emphasize integrating physical, emotional, and spiritual elements in treatment, the more traditional spiritual
focus of *ho'oponopono* may survive.

Another area of wide divergence is the channeling of discussion and
use of *ho'omalu.* Traditionally Hawaiians believed that uncontrolled
emotional expression in *ho'oponopono* exacerbated the problem and
created further *hihia.* Therefore, channeling the discussion was a mechanism to diminish the likelihood of further *hihia.* If that control method
failed, a *ho'omalu* could be used to regain equanimity in the group. As
discussed in an earlier chapter, it may be that the controls in *ho'oponopono* acted as a balance in a society that generally valued expression of
emotions and gregariousness.[2] In contrast, American culture puts a high
premium on direct communication and the control of emotional displays
—particularly fear, sadness, and grief—in day-to-day interaction. Therefore, in therapy, clients in a group situation are often encouraged to
express these emotions and to confront others in a direct way. The differ-

ences in value orientation between Hawaiian and American cultures may account for the differences in use of those related parts in *ho'oponopono*.

One final procedure that is subject to alteration—again due, I believe, to different and changing values—is the phase involving *mihi, kala,* and *oki.* As Pukui et al. (1972, 74) pointed out, in the past individuals were obligated to forgive when asked; a breach of this convention was a grave matter that could incur repercussions from both the family and the ancestral spirits. Ito's study (1978) indicated that today a belief in retribution is still held by urban Hawaiian women. However, Lani Espiritu thought that this belief may not be as strong today as in the past, which may mean that individuals may not feel as motivated to forgive one another.

There is great irony in the conclusion that the distinctively Hawaiian features of *ho'oponopono* are those that are most vulnerable to change since these same features are the ones that many individuals say attract them to this practice. How these crosscurrents will be resolved in the evolution of *ho'oponopono* is still an open question.

The Essence of Ho'oponopono

One of my personal interests in this study was to see if there was any agreement on what constituted the core or essence of *ho'oponopono,* despite the variations. I cannot say I found a phrase or expression that summed up this matter. I did learn that the expression of anything "essential" is always very personal and couched in words and gestures that have individual meanings. In one of the more frivolous moments of an interview I asked Paul Ellis to define "spiritual," since it occurred to me that I had assumed that I shared a similar meaning with him and the others. After Paul gave me an incredulous look and laugh he paraphrased a story reportedly about Louis Armstrong, the legendary jazz musician. "You know Louis was asked, 'What is jazz?' and he replied, 'If you gotta' ask about it, you ain't got it.'" Jazz, spirituality, and the essence of *ho'oponopono* all defy uniform characterization. Yet most people can recognize a quality—the real thing—when it is there.

A few of the leaders in the study shared personal expressions of the essence of *ho'oponopono.* I hope the reader will be able to catch glimmers of the essence of *ho'oponopono* in these words and draw his or her own conclusions.

Jean Baker stated, "The essence of *ho'oponopono,* I think, is *aloha.* That has to be there. And I guess that's manifested in a willingness to contribute some kind of commitment." For Joseph Whitney, the key was "trust" and for Keola Espiritu it was "communication."

Kalau Souza summed up her feelings about *ho'oponopono* by saying, "I think the values Hawaiians have—the sincerity, the commitment to family, commitment to the group—these are all very essential to the whole thing. There's no 'I'm committed, but.' It's 'I'm committed.' Period."

Later in the interview she elaborated:

It's all these things that are so important to the Hawaiian—his God, his feeling of family, the importance of the group. That they're all important to his survival. The commitment to one another, the concern, the real sort of caring. The belief that everything is reciprocal—what you dish out, you get back. Those are all part and parcel of it. When you come here and say you're hurting, you're full up to here, (one can respond) "I know you're suffering, and I, as a part of this family, don't want to see you suffer. And if I can help relieve it in any way, I want to." I think it expresses what *aloha* is. It's the real meaning of *aloha*.

Barriers to Use

With so many positive statements and beliefs about the value of *ho'oponopono,* why do so few people use it? A small number of people have been educated, trained, and encouraged to use it and have not done so. What are their reasons? Aside from one person's statement that he did not use the process because he had not reconciled the spiritual integration, I can only rely on my hunches. As are all family and group therapies, *ho'oponopono* is very complex. It is one thing for a worker to sit down face-to-face with an individual to try and clarify and resolve a difficulty; it is quite another thing to handle the problem in its dynamic and interwoven group context.[3] And, although no one wants to fail or admit failure, our understanding of effective uses of *ho'oponopono* will not be complete until we hear the stories of what did not "work."[4]

Add the Hawaiian cultural form to the complexity of working with a group, and for many counselors and therapists the barriers of family and group work creep higher. The issues may be different for the Hawaiian and the non-Hawaiian. For example, some Hawaiians have a type of reverence toward traditional practices, particularly those that might have been performed by *kahunas,* that precludes them from adapting the practices to contemporary situations. This caution might prevent an otherwise capable leader from using *ho'oponopono.* For a non-Hawaiian there might be a hypersensitivity to possible accusations of "just another damned *haole* trying to rip off the culture." Although both of these examples are forms of stereotypes, as with many stereotypes a grain of truth and legitimate concern are present.

Another probable reason accounting for the scarcity of practitioners is that adequate training and educational opportunities are missing. Currently, materials such as videotapes, discussion guides, and resource books are available for potential users. But alone they do not provide the kind of support and structure necessary to train a cadre of Hawaiian or non-Hawaiian mental health workers. And with current fiscal tightening in social services, it is unlikely that adequate funds will be forthcoming to support such an innovative and possibly controversial training project as ho‘oponopono.

The final concern represents not a barrier to initial use but a barrier to sustained use. When I began the final draft of this work, barely one and a half years after I began the interviews, to the best of my knowledge only two of the eight persons interviewed were still using ho‘oponopono regularly. Neither the drug abuse treatment program nor the wilderness school were still in operation. These programs had accounted for the majority of the leaders. What happened?

Obviously the lack of programmatic context was a major reason, but since most individuals had expressed such positive attitudes toward ho‘oponopono, why didn't they continue to use it in a new setting? Perhaps some are still struggling to find ways of doing this. Other legitimate and worthy reasons for discontinuing use undoubtedly exist. One explanation for the drop in use that occurred to me was that the group as a whole was quite innovative, able to take risks, and able to use an old practice in a new way. A few of the leaders clearly represented the vanguard, while others were just part of a cresting wave by virtue of their situation, or job. Many in this first group of ho‘oponopono users were "movers and shakers" and I suspect it is the nature of movers and shakers to move on. The business of sustaining an innovation is often left to others.

At least one individual continues, with persistence, in a new setting, using ho‘oponopono and lending her efforts to the training of others. The rumblings from this mover and shaker are still perceptible, although how strong and effective they will be in the future is uncertain.

What Do We Have To Gain?

Dr. Haertig's enthusiastic answer to this question of gains in therapy still appeals to me.

> Ho‘oponopono may well be one of the soundest methods to restore and maintain good family relationships that any society has ever devised. (Pukui, Haertig, and Lee 1972, 70)

The Hawaiian family certainly deserves to receive the gifts of its own tradition. Furthermore, study of the transcultural potential of ho‘oponopono could expand our understanding of the uses described in this work and allow for the sharing of this Hawaiian gift. Further study could also shed light on the understanding of therapeutic universals. Finally, a more thorough study of *ho'oponopono* through a comparative, cross-cultural perspective could provide valuable insights into understanding basic principles about assisting people in establishing harmonious interpersonal and social relationships. This task is certainly an essential one for all of us. With a rich variety of tools to use, perhaps we can truly begin to lay a peaceful foundation, beginning with our families, that will heal our vulnerable and conflict-ridden world.

CHAPTER 5 NOTES

1. Two videotapes and an accompanying discussion guide (Shook 1983) are available through the Pacific Basin Family and Children Center at the University of Hawaii Manoa, School of Social Work, Honolulu, Hawaii 96822.

2. Tseng and Hsu (1979) have asserted that therapy can provide a "time out" from normal cultural behavior and expectations.

3. Napier and Whitaker (1978) attest to the difference in how often family therapy is recommended and how often it is actually practiced. They list factors including the complexity and the forbidding costs to the family.

4. See Kopp's *The Naked Therapist* (1976) for refreshing and reassuring reading on therapeutic "worst moments."

Appendix 1

Excerpt on *ho'oponopono* from *Nānā I Ke Kumu,* volume 1, by Mary Kawena Pukui, E. W. Haertig, and Catherine A. Lee (Honolulu: Hui Hānai, 1972), pages 60–70. Reprinted with permission of the Queen Liliuokalani Children's Center.

ho'oponopono *and related concepts.*

ho'oponopono—setting to right; to make right; to correct; to restore and maintain good relationships among family, and family-and-supernatural powers. The specific family conference in which relationships were "set right" through prayer, discussion, confession, repentance, and mutual restitution and forgiveness. This specific practice is discussed here.

> Deriv: *ho'o,* to make, cause or bring about.
> *pono,* correct, right, in perfect order; approximately 20 other closely related meanings.
> *ponopono,* (reduplicate), in order, cared for, attended to. Both forms connote what is socially-morally approved and desirable.

The cassette of the 1971 model tape recorder turned as Mrs. S_____ told this incident of 15 years ago:

"My *hānai* [adoptive] Mom called from the Big Island and said she had a dream that bothered her. She said she had a problem, so better I come home already.

"I said, 'Why don't we talk about it now, over the phone? Maybe I can help you.'

"But Mom said, 'No, better you come home. We need *ho'oponopono*.'
So early next day, I flew home for *ho'oponopono*."

What is this *ho'oponopono*? Why is it important enough to cause
phone calls and plane trips between islands?

As Mary Kawena Pukui describes it:

Ho'oponopono is getting the family together to find out what is
wrong. Maybe to find out why someone is sick, or the cause of a family
quarrel. Then, with discussion and repentance and restitution and forgiveness—and always with prayer—to set right what was wrong.

"to set right" with
each other and God

"*Ho'oponopono* is to set things right with each other and with the
Almighty. I took part in *ho'oponopono* myself for 47 years, from semi-
Christian to Christian times. And whether my *'ohana* [family] prayed to
'aumākua [ancestor gods] or to God, the whole idea of *ho'oponopono*
was the same. Everyone of us searched his heart for hard feelings against
one another. Before God and with His help, we forgave and were forgiven, thrashing out every grudge, peeve or resentment among us."

who took part:
a family matter

Ho'oponopono was essentially a family matter, involving all the
nuclear or immediate family, or only those most concerned with the
problem. Some leeway was possible. A non-relative living with the family
might take part if he was involved with the *pilikia* (trouble). Children
could be excused. And if an involved family member was absent,
ho'oponopono might be held as a "second best" alternative to full family
participation.[1] Though the entire extended family could hold *ho'oponopono,* this was usually impractical. Mrs. Pukui points out that with too
many present, the whole person-to-person interchange of confession-dis-
cussion-forgiveness became impossible. Thus *ho'oponopono* was not a
community-wide therapy. Only the title in its broadest meaning, and
parts of *ho'oponopono,* such as prayer and periods of silence, apply to a
large gathering.

"The ideal," says Mrs. Pukui, "is to keep it in the family and have all
the immediate family taking part."

kahuna or family
senior could lead

Either a helping-healing *kahuna* (but not the *kahuna 'anā'anā* or sorcerer) or a family senior could conduct *ho'oponopono*. In the closely knit

community life of early Hawaii, the *kahuna* usually had a kind of "family doctor" knowledge of a family. This would allow him to lead *ho'oponopono* with real insight into the problems.

From Mrs. Pukui's memories and personal experience, and the shared views and experiences of Hawaiian staff members and associates, we have outlined an "ideal" or "standard" *ho'oponopono*. Basic procedures and therapeutic dynamics are the same, whether the *ho'oponopono* also included traditional-pre-Christian rituals or modern additions.

essentials of
ho'oponopono

This *ho'oponopono* has certain specific requirements. Some concern procedure; others attitudes.

Always included in complete *ho'oponopono* are:

Opening *pule* (prayer) and prayers any time they seem necessary.

A statement of the obvious problem to be solved or prevented from growing worse. This is sometimes called *kūkulu kumuhana* in its secondary meaning.

The "setting to rights" of each successive problem that becomes apparent during the course of *ho'oponopono,* even though this might make a series of *ho'oponoponos* necessary. (This is *mahiki.*)

Self-scrutiny and discussion of individual conduct, attitudes and emotions.

A quality of absolute truthfulness and sincerity. Hawaii called this *'oia'i'o,* the "very spirit of truth."

Control of disruptive emotions by channeling discussion through the leader.

Questioning of involved participants by the leader.

Honest confession to the gods (or God) and to each other of wrongdoing, grievances, grudges and resentments.

Immediate restitution or arrangements to make restitution as soon as possible.

Mutual forgiveness and releasing from the guilts, grudges, and tensions occasioned by the wrong-doing *(hala).* This repenting-forgiving-releasing is embodied in the twin terms, *mihi* and *kala.*

Closing prayer.

Nearly always, the leader called for the periods of silence called *ho'omalu.* Ho'omalu was invoked to calm tempers, encourage self-inquiry into actions, motives and feelings, or simply for rest during an all-day *ho'oponopono.* And once a dispute was settled, the leader decreed *ho'omalu* for the whole subject, both immediately and long after *ho'oponopono* ended.

**pre-Christian
closing rites**

In pre-Christian times, ho'oponopono was followed by pani (closing) rituals. These were usually chicken or pig offerings to the gods. Sometimes pani included the ceremonial ocean bath, kapu kai. Then followed the 'aha 'aina (feast).

Today, post-ho'oponopono rites are virtually unknown. An ordinary meal or a snack usually follows ho'oponopono.

**attitudes needed
in ho'oponopono**

To bring about a true "righting of wrongs," certain attitudes were required. Some concerned the very decision to hold ho'oponopono. For this decision rested on the basic belief that problems could be resolved definitely if they were approached properly. They must be approached with a true intention to correct wrongs. Confession of error must be full and honest. Nothing could be withheld. Prayers, contrition and the forgiving-freeing of kala must come from the heart. Without these, ho'oponopono was form without substance.

**ho'oponopono
for children**

Mrs. Pukui has written a hypothetical ho'oponopono to illustrate basic procedures. In this first quoted excerpt, she combines the opening prayer with statement of the problem.

"I have called you, Pukana, you, Heana, and you, Kahana [all children] to come here and look into this problem with me. Your brother, Kipi, is losing the sight of one eye . . . we want to save the other eye, so that is why we called you together. We will all pray together, and then we'll discuss things.

"Oh, Jehovah God, Creator of heaven and earth, and His Son, Jesus Christ, we ask Your help. To our 'aumākua* from the East and from the West, from the North and from the South, from zenith to horizon, from the upper strata and the lower strata, hearken. Come. We want to discuss together and get your guidance and help, so we can know what is wrong with this boy."

Mrs. Pukui then questioned each child. What came to light first was that Kahana was angry with Kipi over some mischievous prank he had played. This brother-sister disharmony was settled promptly, before any further questioning. Kipi admitted his misbehavior. Then followed the

---

*In an actual pre-Christian ho'oponopono, the 'aumākua would be called on by name —M.K.P.

conceptual ritual of *kala*. This, again geared to the young, went as follows:

Mrs. Pukui: "Kahana, you are willing to *kala* your brother?"
Kahana: "Yes."
Mrs. Pukui: "Free him entirely of this entanglement of your anger?"
Kahana: "Yes."
Mrs. Pukui: "Remember, Kahana, as you loosen your brother from his trespasses, you loosen yourself, too. As you forgive, you are forgiven. Now, who do you want to forgive you?"
Kahana: "Please, God forgive me."
Mrs. Pukui: "Yes, we will ask that now. You gods, hear now that Kahana is to free her brother of his trespasses, and to free him from the crown of his head to the soles of his feet, to the four corners of his body. May he be happy later.
"And you, Kipi, are you willing to *kala* your sister for being angry with you?"
Kipi: "Yes, I am willing."

Nearly identical phrases of *kala* were addressed to Kipi. (The significant use of "free" and "loosen" rather than "forget" is discussed under *kala*.) Then Kipi was questioned more intensively. The boy confessed to stealing some money. He also owned up to an "Hawaiian offense." He had thrown stones at an *'elepaio*, a bird form of a family *'aumakua*. For both, he expressed contrition and asked for forgiveness. Then Mrs. Pukui again prayed.

"To You, O God, and Your sacred Son, and all the *'aumākua* everywhere, hearken to this prayer. This boy is sorry for what he has done. I am sorry he has done such things. So, please free him of his trespasses."

Then followed arrangements for restitution. Kipi was to work at small jobs and earn enough to return the money. His sisters agreed to help him. And to make amends with offended *'aumākua*, he was to offer and burn a food sacrifice *(mōhai 'ai)* of an egg and *ti* leaf. This symbolized the traditional chicken and pig used in *pani* (closing) rites. This settled, Mrs. Pukui concluded:

"Now we dismiss our *ho'oponopono* and we pray that all this trouble be taken away and laid away.

"O, great eyeball of the sun, please take all this bundle of wrongdoing. Take it out to the West with you. And, as you go down again, to your rest, please take all the faults and trespasses that were committed. Lay all of this in the depth of the sea, never more to come back."

Mrs. Pukui's account is an example of *ho'oponopono* in a transition period from Hawaiian to Christian religion. God and the *'aumākua* are invoked impartially. It is rich in Hawaiian concepts: that misconduct was punished by physical illness (the eye ailment); that the body was visualized as having four corners; that the "great eyeball" of the sun held mystic powers, and that mistakes and offenses could be taken away forever in mystic ways. It also illustrates the basic Hawaiian precept that when forgiveness is sincerely asked, it must be granted.

Because this *ho'oponopono* concerned children, it did not include the emotional depth, self-scrutiny of motives, guilts and aggressions, and the periods of silence *(ho'omalu)* of an adult session. In fact, Mrs. Pukui says that,

"In my grandmother's home, small children always sat in on *ho'o-ponopono* even if they didn't take part. Many times I was even bored, until I grew to understand better. . . ."[2]

ho'oponopono
for Mrs. S_____

The adult subtleties of guilt and remorse were very much present in the *ho'oponopono* mentioned in the beginning of this discussion. This is the one so urgently requested by the *hānai* mother of Mrs. S_____. Mrs. S_____ continues with her recorded account:

"So I took my baby with me, and went home to Kona the next day. All the family were there. My *hānai* cousin's Mom—she is a lady minister—was there to lead *ho'oponopono*.

(From here on, the minister is referred to as "This Lady" or *"ho'ōla"* literally "healer," but more generally used to mean a minister, often believed to have gifts of healing or prophecy.)

"My *hānai* Mom was in bed. They told me Mom had felt very sick and had gone to the doctor. She was 69. And she felt that some of her sickness was really physical. Some of it—well, maybe not. Then she had this dream. And then she knew I should come home and all of us should *ho'oponopono*.

"So we all got together in the living room. No, not kneeling down. Just comfortable. Not a real circle, but so we could see each other.

wehe i ka
Paipala

"First This Lady prayed, all in Hawaiian* . . . asking Jehovah God to show us His word and how to find out what was wrong. How to help Mom get well. And while This Lady prayed, Mom opened the Bible for guidance. (This was *wehe i ka Paipala*. . . .)

---

*Everyone present understood Hawaiian. Intelligibility throughout is a requirement of effective *ho'oponopono*.

"Then Mom told her dream. She dreamed that I was alongside a high cliff and I was about to fall in the ocean. So Mom yelled. But when she yelled out at me, I said, 'Oh, I'm going.' And the second and the third time, she called me, and I said, 'I'm going.' And Mom said she thought this dream meant that because I was living in Honolulu I was *ho'okano* [conceited] and I didn't take any interest in her or her welfare. I thought, because of Mom's age and all, she just wanted attention.

"But This Lady, the *ho'ōla*, she thought the dream and my Mom's sickness meant that Mom was holding something back.* Something that she had not let me know.

old wrong &
guilt emerge

"So This Lady prayed again. And we all kept quiet for a while . . . trying to help Mom. And then Mom told us more. . . . She said that before my grandmother died, she gave her [Mom] a Hawaiian quilt. Mom was supposed to give it to me when I grew up. It was really my quilt, meant for me.

"But my *hānai* Mom kept it. And when I grew up and got married, she never gave me that quilt. Others, but not this one. What happened was that Mom sold the quilt for $300. And she had been living with all this *'ike hewa* [guilt] all this time. This Lady said part of Mom's sickness was because of this guilt. She told Mom she would never get well until she got my forgiveness. And Mom cried. She really cried! She felt so guilty.

confession &
forgiveness

"Then the *ho'ōla* said Mom should confess to me and before God Jehovah. She did. She asked me to forgive her, and I did. I wasn't angry. . . . And later Mom's sickness left her. Of course, she still had diabetes, but the rest—being so confused and miserable—all that left her."

Interviewer: "But what about your quilt? Did she arrange for any restitution?"

restitution
was made

Mrs. S: "Oh, yes. During *ho'oponopono* she said she would quilt another one for me. The others helped her. She got the quilt finished and gave it to me before she died."

Interviewer: "How did you end *ho'oponopono?*"

---

*Dreams are commonly prompted by something repressed, comments the Center's psychiatrist. The *ho'ōla*, also a relative, was able to draw on long knowledge of family affairs.

next problem
is dealt with
Mrs. S: "We didn't end it right away. We had to work more on the dream.
You know, the dream where Mom saw me on the *pali* not paying any
attention to her calls. Well, This Lady, she interpreted this to mean that
because my *hānai* Mom had done this thing about the quilt and kept it
a secret, this was really why I would not answer. And why I ignore
Mom in real life. But I said, 'No, I am not ignoring Mom. It is just that
I am married now and have a baby and I am busy.' But Mom said that I
did neglect her. That I did not write home, sometimes for a long time.
And the *ho'ōla* told me, 'After this, you should write often. Your
mother is old, and she needs your letters. She looks forward to hearing
from you.' And Mom cried again. And I felt, oh, so much love for her.
"And we talked about, oh, lots of little misunderstandings. And we
forgave each other for so many things. The *ho'oponopono* brought us
so close together. It did. It really did! And we stayed close to each other
until the very day Mom died.

closing
prayer
"Then the Lady prayed again to Jehovah God, thanking Him for opening up the way and giving us an answer. And she thanked Jehovah for
bringing things out in the clear. She prayed to Jehovah to close the
doors, so no evil in the family or from outside would harm us . . . she
asked the angels of Jehovah God to guard the four posts of the house.
Then she *amen'd** all in Hawaiian.
"And after *ho'oponopono,* it was so peaceful-like. There was love—
oh, so much love!"

Interviewer: "How long was this last prayer?"
Mrs. S: "About half an hour."
Interviewer: "How long was the *ho'oponopono?*"
Mrs. S: "Oh, all day. One person took care of the phone so we
   wouldn't be interrupted."
Interviewer: "After it ended, what did you do?"
Mrs. S: "We were hungry. We ate. Just supper—not a special meal."

alcohol is
not allowed
Interviewer: "I know that you, personally, do not drink. But could
   anyone else have had a highball or a beer during the day?"

---

*In this case, the Christian "Amen" has been used as a verb. In pre-Christian Hawaii, pray-
ers and chants were concluded with phrases using *'āmama,* meaning "the prayer is free" or
"flown" or "finished."

Mrs. S: "Oh, No! Nobody ever drinks in *ho'oponopono*. Because when people drink they let their feelings, their temper run away from them. In our *ho'oponopono*, we cried a lot when we forgave and made up, but we had to stay in control. I mean over really strong feelings like anger."

Mrs. S_____'s account and Mrs. Pukui's earlier example show some interesting similarities and differences. Both point out one of the common traditional reasons for *ho'oponopono*, that of finding the cause of a puzzling illness. Said Mrs. S_____, "A part of Mom's illness was physical . . . but part of it, well maybe not." A century ago, *kahunas* often asked "has the *ho'oponopono* been held?" before they would proceed with treatment. And on Niihau today, families hold *ho'oponopono* first, then call Kauai for medical help if the illness persists.

mahiki, layers
beneath layers

Both examples demonstrate *mahiki,* the dealing with each successive "layer" of trouble, one at a time. In the *ho'oponopono* for childhood transgression, these layers were of easily recognized conduct and emotion. First, childish misbehavior and the anger it caused, then the theft, then throwing stones at the *'elepaio* bird—all were brought out in turn. In the adult *ho'oponopono*, the layers were made also of emotion-underlying-emotion. Let's trace the structure of this disturbed relationship.

To borrow medical terms, the "presenting complaints" were a dream and an illness. At first, only the "top layer" of dream significance was discussed. It, said the *ho'ōla*, like the illness, meant "Mom is holding something back."

What was she holding back?

A hostile act, that of selling the quilt. This caused long-standing guilt. And this guilt was a factor causing Mom to accompany and complicate organic disorders with functional or psychosomatic illness.

How were these revealed layers "disposed of"?

For Mom, confession, discussion, restitution and expressed contrition. For mother and daughter, mutual forgiving and releasing (*mihi* and *kala*). All in the presence of God.

But was *mahiki* complete? All layers stripped away?

Not yet, there was more to the dream. As the *ho'ōla* interpreted it, the mother's hostile action (in dream form, placing daughter on the dangerous cliff) led to lack of communication between mother and daughter (daughter-in-dream refused to answer mother's calls). As Mom saw it, daughter ignored her from general selfishness and haughtiness exemplified in the move to Honolulu.

And, on the conscious level were actual instances of daughter's neglect and the mother's resentment of this neglect. These layers also must be taken care of. And yet more "layers" were peeled off and dissolved in discussion, in *mihi* and *kala*—and in tears and embraces.

("And we talked about so many little misunderstandings. And we forgave each other for so many things.")

Or, as Mrs. Pukui describes the abstract in terms of the tangible, "Think of peeling an onion. You peel off one layer and throw it aside, so you can go on and peel off the next layer. That's *mahiki.*"

ho'omalu and
kūkulu kumuhana

In Mrs. S_____'s experience, two more components of *ho'oponopono* seem to have come into being spontaneously and simultaneously.

"Then we all kept quiet awhile . . . trying to help Mom," Mrs. S_____ relates.

We could rephrase it as:

"We all kept quiet awhile." Or, "We all had *ho'omalu*" (a period of silence for thought and reflection).

". . . trying to help Mom." Or, ". . . and we joined in *kūkulu kumuhana*" (the pooling of emotional-spiritual forces for a common purpose).*

The *ho'ōla* in this *ho'oponopono* did not need to control temper outbursts. ("I wasn't angry," said Mrs. S_____.)

the leader
intervenes

In a more recent *ho'oponopono,* the leader did intervene frequently. This *ho'oponopono* concerned primarily "Dan," his *hapa-haole*† wife, "Relana," and Dan's mother. Mother and daughter-in-law had been increasingly hostile ever since the young couple married. As time went on, in-laws on both sides were drawn into the family *hihia* (entanglement of ill-feeling). Finally, after eight years, Dan pursuaded his wife and mother to join him in *ho'oponopono.* Dan's great-aunt conducted it. As resentments and bitterness were brought out, open accusations were made.

"You never made me welcome at your house," charged mother-in-law.

"You never came to visit. Just to interfere," said daughter-in-law.

"I wanted to show you how to cook right. But would you let me teach you anything? Not you! *Ho'okano!*"

As voices rose, *Tūtū* ("Auntie") called for *ho'omalu.* Then after a min-

---

*Both *ho'omalu* and *kūkulu kumuhana* are discussed at end of *ho'oponopono* listing.
†half-Hawaiian; half-Caucasian.

ute or two of silence, she insisted each one must talk in turn, to her, not to each other.

"She laid down the law several times," Dan reports, "but in the end the two got down to talking about *why* they were angry, instead of just yelling at each other."

What gradually emerged then was a young, mainland-educated wife's attempts to be independent and to fashion her household along "modern" lines, and a Hawaiian mother-in-law's clinging both to her son and to Hawaiian traditions of close-knit family relationships and living patterns.

"It was a long, long *ho'oponopono*. Relana and Mom must have *mihi'd* and *kala'd* a dozen times. They never will see eye-to-eye. But we do visit back and forth now and we all get along pretty well," states Dan.

"Now we're trying to get all the others—all the in-laws—to *ho'oponopono* to straighten out the rest of the *hihia*."

Intervention by the leader anytime it was needed was traditional, says Mrs. Pukui.

"The leader had complete authority. When he said '*Pau*. Enough of this.' everybody got quiet. Sometimes the leader would stop the talk because of hot tempers. Sometimes, if he thought someone was not being honest, or holding things back, or making up excuses instead of facing up to his own *hala* [fault]. Then the leader would ask the person, '*Heaha kau i hana ai? What did you really do? Ho'o mao popo*. Think about it.' And there would be *ho'omalu* for a little while."

emotions kept
under control

Obviously, a successful *ho'oponopono* was not mere emotional catharsis. Hawaiians seemed to know that neither crying jag nor shouting match solves a problem.

In fact, the Center's psychiatric consultant believes the emotional controls of *ho'oponopono* provide one of its great therapeutic strengths. To quote:

"In *ho'oponopono*, one talked openly *about* one's feelings, particularly one's angers and resentments. This is good. For when you suppress asnd repress hostilities, pretend they do not exist, then sooner or later they are going to burst out of containment, often in destructive, damaging ways. *Ho'oponopono* used the 'safety valve' of discussion as one step towards handling old quarrels or grudges, and even more importantly, as prevention, so minor disputes would not grow into big grievances.

"But 'talking things out' is not enough. Something constructive must be done about the cause of the grudge, the reasons behind the quarrel. And to get this done, talking about anger must be kept under control. Let the anger itself erupt anew, and more causes for more resentments build up. 'Setting things to rights' requires all the maturity one can muster. When run-away emotions take over, so do child-like attitudes and behavior. The *ho'oponopono* provision that participants talk about anger to the leader, rather than hurling maledictions at each other was a wise one.

"Only when people control their hostile emotions can satisfactory means of restitution be worked out. And usually, it's pretty hard to forgive fully and freely until, for example, property has been returned or damage repaired or one's good name has been cleared.

"*Ho'oponopono* seems to be a supreme effort at self-help on a responsible, adult level. It also has the spiritual dimension so vital to the Hawaiian people. And even here, prayers, to *'aumākua* in the past or God in the present, are responsible, adult prayers. The appeal is not the child-like, 'Rescue me! Get me out of this scrape.' Rather it is, 'Please provide the spiritual strength we need to work out this problem. Help us to help ourselves.'"

ho'oponopono
defined in 1971

Unfortunately, very few Hawaiians practice this "supreme effort at self-help" in 1971. For when Christianity came in, more than a century ago, *ho'oponopono* went out. Because *ho'oponopono* prayers and rituals were addressed to "pagan gods," the *akua* and *'aumākua,* the total *ho'oponopono* was labeled "pagan." Many Hawaiians came to believe their time honored method of family therapy was "a stupid, heathen thing." Some practiced *ho'oponopono* secretly. As time went on, Hawaiians remembered not *ho'oponopono* but only bits and pieces of it. Or grafted-on innovations. Or mutations. Or complete distortions of concept, procedure and vocabulary.

In the past five years, Center staff members have compiled an almost unbelievable list of incomplete or distorted explanations of what *ho'oponopono* is. Most—but not all—come from clients. Here are the most typical examples:

Fortune-telling was called *ho'oponopono.* So were unintelligible rituals: "This lady prayed over me—I think in Portuguese." "The *kahuna* prayed in Hawaiian, so low I didn't know what he was saying." "I went to this man and he chanted something."

A self-styled *"kahuna"* offered to kill by sorcery (evidently *ho'opi-'opi'o)* and this was called *ho'oponopono.*

The Mormon Family Circle, and any family discussion were termed *ho'oponopono.*

Many Hawaiians called family prayers *(pule 'ohana) ho'oponopono.*

One client said *ho'oponopono* was "fasting and praying three days";

another said it meant "blessing the house" and "casting out demons"; others said it meant "reading the Bible" and "forgiving each other."

A non-client viewed *ho'oponopono* as "arbitration by a senior."

By far the most common comment was that *wehe i ka Paipala,* often a modern prelude, was in itself *ho'oponopono.*

Probably the most widespread departure from the "classic" or "model" is using *ho'oponopono* concepts and procedures in a church group with a minister as leader. In this, the family participation restriction is extended to take in "spiritual family."

true ho'oponopono:
the sum of its parts

Many of these fragments, innovations, additions or departures are themselves desirable. The point is they are not *ho'oponopono* in its entirety. For Hawaii's family therapy is the sum total of many parts: prayer, discussion, arbitration, contrition, restitution, forgiveness and releasing, and the thorough looking into layers of action and feeling called *mahiki.* It is this sum total of its many beneficial parts that makes *ho'oponopono* a useful, effective method to remedy and even prevent family discord.

Or, as Dr. Haertig states:

"*Ho'oponopono* may well be one of the soundest methods to restore and maintain good family relationships that any society has ever devised."

NOTES

1. *Ho'oponopono* with involved member absent. Shortly before this went to press, the following account was received: John H. of Oahu was seriously ill and his own family planned *ho'oponopono* to find the cause. His estranged wife, Melea, on Maui, flatly refused to attend and said she would "never forgive John for cheating on me." John's family went ahead with a kind of "second best" *ho'oponopono.* Mutual forgiving-releasing was obviously impossible. However, John did confess and talk about his past infidelities and present hostilities. His family told him these were at the root of his illness. Whether or not this was a case of simply treating psychosomatic symptoms, we don't know. However, the report says John then recovered. Almost a year later, the same family members— but not John—went to Maui. There they held a long-delayed *ho'oponopono* with Melea to "cleanse her heart of all her hates." In this *ho'oponopono* a decision was reached. Reconciliation would never work. Melea should, with full family approval, divorce John. She did this.

This is an interesting example of two *ho'oponopono* (or one *ho'oponopono* in a delayed series) to deal with the total John-Melea problem. The decision for divorce when John and Melea could and would not sincerely forgive and release each other of guilts and resentments has interesting traditional precedent. In Hawaii of old, couples could *'oki* (sever) marriage arrangements. When any family discord was clearly irreparable, the family tie could be formally broken. This was expressed in the ritual term, *mō ka piko, mōku ka piko* ("The umbilical cord is cut.").

2. Children present at *ho'oponopono*. This was in keeping with Hawaiian involvement of children in nearly every aspect of family life. Little effort was made to shield children from the "realities of life" as Western society, for example, does this today. In old Hawaii, children learned skills by watching their elders; grew to know about death and sorrow by attending wakes and funerals and touching the corpse. Sexual information was not withheld; though women went into isolation during menstruation, even little boys knew *why* their mother was isolated. Childhood attendance at *ho'oponopono* not only gave lessons in how to conduct one in future adult life, it accomplished a more immediate purpose: that of letting children know that adults had problems, lost their tempers, and committed wrongs—and were willing to talk about them and find ways to resolve conflicts and improve conduct.

Appendix 2

Ho'oponopono Interview

FACE SHEET
1. Name
2. Date
3. Place of interview
4. Sex
5. Age
6. Ethnicity (self-defined)
7. Education
8. Training (social work, education, counseling)
9. Place of residence
10. Length of residence in Hawaii
11. Place where reared
12. Occupation
13. Religion
14. Personal/family values

NOTES:

*The primary purpose of this guide was to ensure that the interviewer had some specific knowledge about the subject prior to doing the interviews. The guide was not given to the respondents nor in most cases was it used to structure the interviews. It acted as a checklist for items to be covered and a guide to formulating effective probes of respondents' statements. The use of the guide changed over the course of the interviews as some categories were not found to be particularly useful.

GUIDE

A. MEANING OF *HO'OPONOPONO*

1. What is the purpose (prevention? intervention?)?

2. Who are the participants?

   a) What is the role of the leader?

   b) What are the roles of the others?

   c) What is the group size?

   d) Is participation voluntary or mandatory?

3. How is *ho'oponopono* convened?

   a) Who decides when *ho'oponopono* takes place?

   b) What kind of decision is used (consensus, majority, one person)?

   c) Are sessions spontaneous/scheduled? or both?

4. How are participants prepared?

   a) Are participants educated about *ho'oponopono?*

   b) Do participants contract or make agreements?

   c) Is there an explanation of purpose, roles, expectations, procedures?

   d) Is confidentiality discussed?

5. Prerequisite beliefs and values (Are there any? Are they seen as important?)

   a) Are there meaningful interpersonal relationships among participants?

      1) Do the individuals live together?

2) Are participants related?

3) Do the participants do something together consistently that would result in a valued relationship?

b) Are there common values? (such as:)

1) Interdependence

2) Concern for group over individual

3) Expressing feelings

4) Truthfulness

5) Sincerity

6) Patience

c) What are the common beliefs? (regarding:)

1) The nature and effect of conflict (Is there a recognition of loss if conflict is not resolved? Retribution?)

2) Spiritual matters

d) Is there a high level of group trust?

e) Is there an awareness of the effect of an individual's actions on the group?

f) Are there ethnocultural commonalities in the group?

6. Beginning phase (Are the following steps included? If yes, how are they conducted?)

a) Prayer (silence, or opening statement for assistance?)
pule

b) General problem identification
kūkulu kumuhana

c) Zeroing in on the specific problem
mahiki

hala

hihia

7. Resolution phase (Are the following procedures included? If yes, how are they handled?)

a) Self-scrutiny

b) Questioning by the leader

c) Sharing one's feelings (and who shares)
mana'o

d) All discussion channeled by the leader

e) Leader prevents emotional outbursts
ho'omalu

f) Confession of wrongdoing
mihi

g) Forgiveness
kala

oki

h) Recognition of grudge holding
ho'omauhala

i) Restitution

8. Closing phase (Are the following procedures included? If yes, how are they handled?)

a) Summary

b) Reaffirmation of positive group relations

c) Problem declared closed; reaffirmation that the hurt has been resolved

d) Prayer
pule ho'opau

e) Closing the problem
pani

f) Closing the *ho'oponopono* sessions
final *pani*

g) Sharing snack or meal (at end of each session and at final closing)

9. Other notes

a) Is there a distinction between single *ho'oponopono* sessions when an entire series of problems can be resolved in one time period and those complex conditions/problems that require a series of sessions over a period of time?

b) Does the process of problem identification and resolution usually repeat itself several times within one session before the closing?

10. How much time is allowed for sessions?

11. What is the emotional climate throughout?

B. DECISION TO ADOPT

1. How did the leader learn about *ho'oponopono?*

a) Literature (books, magazines, newspapers)

b) Formal presentation (school, workshop)

c) Informal, face-to-face

2. How did the leader acquire the skill of using *ho'oponopono?*

a) Reading

b) Training

c) Observing

d) Participating

3. How does it fit with other agency functions/programs?

a) What is the purpose of the agency?

b) Is its use a policy decision or an agency practice?

4. How was the decision to adopt made?

a) Was it an individual or group decision?

b) What is the perceived purpose it serves in the agency?

c) Were other alternative methods considered? (and what were they?)

C. ASSESSMENT

1. How does the agency/individual judge whether or not using *ho'oponopono* is meeting the desired goals and objectives?

a) Are there:
   1) Documents/reports?

   2) Statistical measures?

b) If yes, what are the results? (attach, if necessary)

2. Is it being used on a trial basis?

a) If yes:
   1) Why?

   2) How long?

3. Is it part of a time-limited project (i.e., private or government funding)?

4. If it were to be discontinued, who would make the decision and on what basis?

5. What difficulties were encountered using it?

6. Did the agency or individual have access to a resource person to assist them in evaluating or in helping to iron out any difficulties encountered?

7. What suggestions would be made to others who wanted to use it?
   a) Specific—*ho'oponopono*

   b) General—recommendations about adopting/adapting indigenous practices

Glossary of Hawaiian Terms

The primary references for these terms are Pukui, Elbert, and Mookini (1975) and Pukui, Haertig, and Lee (1972).

Ali'i. Traditional Hawaiian chief system.

Aloha. Love, a greeting of hello or good-bye, compassion.

Aloha 'āina. Love of the land.

'Aumākua. Family or personal gods. Seen as spiritual ancestors who may still be part of the *'ohana*. The *'aumākua* provide both protection and warnings to the family. They also mediate between the person and other impersonal gods, the *akua*.

Haku. Literally, lord, master, owner. In *ho'oponopono* the *haku* is the leader who facilitates and guides the session.

Hala. Fault, error, transgression. In *ho'oponopono* the *hala* is identified as the source of the *hihia*. The transgression binds the wrongdoer to the wronged like a cord.

Hānai. Adopted child. Adoption was and is fairly common. Although it may not be done formally via the legal system, a *hānai* situation is considered permanent. The *hānai* child is taken, usually by grandparents or other relatives, to be loved, nourished, and educated.

Haole. Generally refers to Caucasians; originally meant foreigner.

Hele. To go, come. *Hele on.* Let's get going; get on with it.

Hihia. Entanglement. In *ho'oponopono* the *hihia* represents the complex net of problems that usually involves a number of members in the family.

Ho'ohiki. Vow, promise, binding oath.

Ho'okeai. Fasting; sometimes used to induce spiritual guidance.

Ho'omalu. From *ho'o* (to cause or make) and *malu* (shade, peace, protection). In *ho'oponopono* a *ho'omalu* may be called to provide a cooling-off period for the participants when emotional displays are disruptive; can be an injunction to let the troubles discussed in the session remain confidential, unspoken, laid to rest.

Ho'omauhala. To hold onto the fault; to hold a grudge. Sometimes in *ho'oponopono* a person is unable to forgive and release. A *ho'omalu* may be called. Traditionally, if a person was unable to forgive, it was considered a grave offense.

Ho'oponopono. To set right; a process for restoring harmonious relations in the family.

Hui. Club, partnership, association.

Hula. Hawaiian dance.

Kahuna. Priest, minister, healer, sorcerer, specialist.

Kahuna lapa'au. Medical practitioner.

Kala. To loosen until free. In *ho'oponopono* the *mihi* by one person is responded to by a *kala* from another, releasing the two from the negative entanglement that has bound them together.

Kōkua. Help, assistance, cooperation.

Kūkulu kumuhana. The pooling of strengths for a shared purpose. In *ho'oponopono* it is also the statement of the problem or reaching out to a person who is resisting the process.

Kumu. Teacher, manual, primer, source of knowledge.

Kūpuna. Grandparent, ancestor. The *kūpuna* (plural form) are respected and revered for their knowledge and wisdom.

Laulima. Cooperation; joining together to accomplish a project or job.

Lono. God of agriculture and the harvest festivities; one of the four major Hawaiian gods.

Lū'au. A Hawaiian feast.

Maha'oi. Bold, inquisitive, rude behavior.

Mahiki. To peel off. In *ho'oponopono* the *mahiki* is the discussion phase that allows the layers of the problem to be dealt with and peeled off one layer at a time.

Mana'o. Thought, idea, opinion. Connotes sincere expression.

Mihi. To confess, apologize, to be sorry. The *mihi* is an important step in the resolution phase during *ho'oponopono*.

Mo ka piko. Literally, to sever the umbilical cord. In *ho'oponopono* this means to sever ties with a family member because of a serious threatening offense such as *ho'omauhala*.

Noho. Hypnotic trance state; possession syndrome.

'Oha. Taro.

'Ohana. Family. Often refers to the extended family of grandparents, aunts, uncles, cousins, nieces, nephews, and others. Used contemporarily to identify a family-like bond that exists among group members.

Oki. To sever, to cut. In *ho'oponopono* the *mihi* and *kala* are made complete by the *oki,* showing that the entanglement and the troubles are really settled and released.

Pani. To close, shut. The family may share a snack or meal to close the *ho'oponopono.*

Pau. Finished, closed, complete.

Pilikia. Trouble, nuisance, tragedy.

Pule. Prayer. Used to open and close *ho'oponopono* sessions and to mark many other occasions.

Pule ho'opau. Closing prayer. In *ho'oponopono* this can be a statement of thanks and a reaffirmation of family bonds.

Tūtū (actual Hawaiian spelling *kūkū*). An affectionate term for grandmother or grandfather; used more loosely to refer to anyone of a grandparent's generation.

'Ukulele. Literally, "leaping flea." Generally known as a small, four-string guitar of Portuguese origin.

Ukupau. To pay for a completed job rather than for work done by the hour. Also used colloquially for work that everyone pitches in to accomplish early.

Wehe wehe. To open, untie. Used in this work to signify discussion that reaches below the superficial level.

References

Abad, V., J. Ramos, and E. Boyce
1974 A model for delivery of mental health services to Spanish-speaking minorities. *American Journal of Orthopsychiatry* 44:584–595.

Adler, P.
1974 Beyond cultural identity: reflections upon cultural and multicultural man. *Topics in Culture Learning* 2:23–40.

Atkinson, D., G. Morten, and D. W. Sue, eds.
1979 *Counseling American Minorities.* Dubuque, Iowa: Wm. C. Brown Company.

Bandler, R., and J. Grinder
1976 *The Structure of Magic,* 2 vols. Palo Alto: Science and Behavior Books.

Barnett, H.
1953 *Innovation: The Basis of Cultural Change.* New York: McGraw-Hill.

Bogdan, R., and S. J. Taylor
1975 *Introduction to Qualitative Research Methods: A Phenomenological Approach to the Social Sciences.* New York: John Wiley and Sons.

Boggs, S., K. Watson-Gegeo, and G. McMillan
1985 *Speaking, Relating and Learning: A Study of Hawaiian Children at Home and at School.* Norwood, New Jersey: Ablex Publishing Company.

Brown, T., K. Stein, K. Huang, and D. Harris
1973 Mental illness and the role of mental health facilities in Chinatown. In *Asian Americans: Psychological Perspectives,* ed. S. Sue and N. Wagner, 221–231. Palo Alto: Science and Behavior Books.

Bryson, S., and H. Bardo
1979 Race and the counseling process. In *Counseling American Minorities,* ed. D. Atkinson, G. Morten, and D. W. Sue, 122–132. Dubuque, Iowa: Wm. C. Brown Company.

Bulhan, H. A.
  1980   Dynamics of cultural in-betweenity: an empirical study. *International
          Journal of Psychology* 15 (July): 105–121.

Christensen, E. W.
  1979   Counseling Puerto Ricans: some considerations. In *Counseling Ameri-
          can Minorities,* ed. D. Atkinson, G. Morten, and D. W. Sue, 159–
          167. Dubuque, Iowa: Wm. C. Brown Company.

Cottle, T. J.
  1977   *Private Lives, Public Accounts.* Amherst, Massachusetts: University of
          Massachusetts Press.

Delgado, M.
  1982   Cultural consultation: implications for Hispanic mental health ser-
          vices in the United States. *International Journal of Intercultural Rela-
          tions* 6:227–250.

Draguns, J.
  1975   Resocialization into culture: the complexities of taking a worldwide
          view of psychotherapy. In *Cross-Cultural Perspectives on Learning,*
          ed. R. Brislin, S. Bochner, and W. Lonner, 227–289. New York: John
          Wiley and Sons.

  1981a   Cross-cultural counseling and psychotherapy: history, issues and cur-
          rent status. In *Cross-Cultural Counseling and Psychotherapy,* ed.
          A. Marsella and P. Pedersen, 3–27. New York: Pergamon Press.

  1981b   Counseling across cultures: common themes and distinct approaches.
          In *Counseling Across Cultures,* ed. P. Pedersen, J. Draguns, W. Lon-
          ner, and J. Trimble, 3–21. Honolulu: University Press of Hawaii.

Edwards, E. D., and M. E. Edwards
  1980   American Indians: working with individuals and groups. *Social Case-
          work* 6 (October): 498–506.

Fields, S.
  1979   Mental health and the melting pot. *Innovations* 6:2.

Frank, J.
  1961   *Persuasion and Healing: A Comparative Study of Psychotherapy.* Bal-
          timore: Johns Hopkins University Press.

  1971   Therapeutic factors in psychotherapy. *American Journal of Psy-
          chotherapy* 25:350–361.

Gallimore, R., J. Boggs, and C. Jordan
  1974   *Culture, Behavior and Education: A Study of Hawaiian Americans.*
          Beverly Hills: Sage Publications.

Garrison, V.
  1978   Support systems of schizophrenic and nonschizophrenic Puerto Rican
          women in New York city. *Schizophrenia Bulletin* 4:561–596.

Geertz, C.
  1973   *The Interpretation of Cultures.* New York: Basic Books, Inc.

Glaser, B., and A. Strauss
  1967   *The Discovery of Grounded Theory: Strategies for Qualitative Re-
          search.* New York: Aldine Publishing Company.

Gonzales, E.
1976　The role of Chicano folk beliefs and practices in mental health. In *Chicanos: Social and Psychological Perspectives,* ed. C. Hernandez, M. Haug, and N. Wagner, 236–281. St. Louis: C. V. Mosby Company.

Handy, E., and M. Pukui
1972　*The Polynesian Family System of Ka'u Hawaii.* Tokyo: Charles E. Tuttle Company.

Hawaii. Department of Planning and Economic Development
1983　*The State of Hawaii Data Book.*

Higginbotham, H.
1976　A conceptual model for the delivery of psychological services. *Topics in Culture Learning* 4:44–52.

1979　Culture and mental health services. In *Perspectives on Cross-Cultural Psychology,* ed. A. Marsella, R. Tharp, and T. Ciborowski, 307–332. New York: Academic Press.

Honolulu Sunday Star-Bulletin and Advertiser
1971　Ho'oponopono: a way to set things right. July 18, B-8.

Howard, A.
1974　*Ain't No Big Thing: Coping Strategies in a Hawaiian-American Community.* Honolulu: University Press of Hawaii.

Hunt, W., W. Crane, and J. Wahlke
1964　Interviewing political elites in cross-cultural comparative research. *American Journal of Sociology* 70:59–68.

Ito, K.
1978　Symbolic conscience: illness retribution among urban Hawaiian women. Ph.D. dissertation in anthropology, University of California, Los Angeles.

1982　Illness as retribution: a cultural form of self-analysis among urban Hawaiian women. *Culture, Medicine and Psychiatry* 6:385–403.

Ivey, A.
1981　Counseling and psychotherapy: toward a new perspective. In *Cross-Cultural Counseling and Psychotherapy,* ed. A. Marsella and P. Pedersen, 279–311. New York: Pergamon Press.

Ivey, A., and J. Authier
1971　*Microcounseling.* Springfield, Illinois: Charles C. Thomas.

Kahn, M., C. Williams, E. Galvez, L. Lejero, R. Conrad, and G. Goldstein
1975　The Papago Psychology Service: a community mental health program on an American Indian reservation. *American Journal of Community Psychology* 3:81–97.

Kanahele, G.
1982　*Hawaiian Renaissance.* Hawaiian Values, Series I (pamphlet). Honolulu: WAIHA.

Kiev, A.
1964　*Magic, Faith and Healing.* New York: The Free Press.

Kimura, L.
1983   Native Hawaiian culture: language. In *Native Hawaiian Study Commission Report* 1:191.

Kitano, H., and N. Matsushima
1981   Counseling Asian Americans. In *Counseling Across Cultures,* ed. P. Pedersen, J. Draguns, W. Lonner, and J. Trimble, 163–180. Honolulu: University Press of Hawaii.

Kleinman, A.
1980   *Patients and Healers in the Context of Culture.* Berkeley: University of California Press.

Kluckholn, C.
1962   *Culture and Behavior.* New York: The Free Press.

Kopp, S.
1976   *The Naked Therapist.* San Diego: EDITS.

Kroeber, A., and C. Kluckholn
1952   Culture: a critical review of concepts and definitions. Cambridge, Massachusetts: Papers of the Peabody Museum 47 (1).

Lebra, W.
1976   *Culture-Bound Syndromes, Ethnopsychiatry and Alternate Therapies.* Honolulu: University Press of Hawaii.

Lefley, H., and R. Urrutia
1982   Final report—cross-cultural training for mental health personnel. Department of Psychiatry, University of Miami School of Medicine.

Lewis, R., and M. Ho
1979   Social work with Native Americans. In *Counseling American Minorities,* ed. D. Atkinson, G. Morten, and D. W. Sue, 51–58. Dubuque, Iowa: Wm. C. Brown Company.

Lofland, J.
1971   *Analyzing Social Settings.* Belmont, California: Wadsworth Publishing Company, Inc.

1976   *Doing Social Life.* New York: John Wiley and Sons.

MacDonald, W., and C. Oden, Jr.
1977   Aumakua: behavioral direction visions in Hawaiians. *Journal of Abnormal Psychology* 86 (2): 189–194.

Marsella, A.
1980   Culture and mental health: some contributions of cross-cultural research. Paper presented at the Conference on Cultural Aspects of Mental Health and Therapy, Honolulu, Hawaii.

1982   Culture and mental health: an overview. In *Cultural Conceptions of Mental Health and Therapy,* ed. A. Marsella and G. White, 359–389. Boston: D. Reidel Publishing Company.

Marsella, A., and G. White, eds.
1982   *Cultural Conceptions of Mental Health and Therapy.* Boston: D. Reidel Publishing Company.

McDermott, J., W. S. Tseng, and T. W. Maretzki
1980   *People and Cultures of Hawaii.* Honolulu: University Press of Hawaii.

McMakin, P.
1975   The suruhanos: traditional curers on the island of Guam. M.A. thesis, University of Guam.

Mossman, M., and P. Wahilani
1975   Kulia i lokahi i ke ola! (Mimeographed)

Murase, T.
1982   Sunao: a central value in Japanese psychotherapy. In *Cultural Conceptions of Mental Health and Therapy*, ed. A. Marsella and G. White, 317–329. Boston: D. Reidel Publishing Company.

Napier, A., and C. Whitaker
1978   *The Family Crucible*. New York: Harper and Row.

Nishihara, D.
1978   Culture, counseling and ho'oponopono: an ancient model in a modern context. *Personnel and Guidance Journal* (May): 56–62.

Paglinawan, L.
1972   Ho'oponopono project II. (Unpublished document of limited circulation.) Honolulu: Hawaiian Culture Committee, Queen Liliuokalani Children's Center.

1980   Untitled paper. University of Hawaii School of Social Work. (Mimeographed)

Pareek, U., and T. Venkateswara Rao
1980   Cross-cultural surveys and interviewing. In *Handbook of Cross-Cultural Psychology*, ed. H. Triandis and J. Draguns, 2:127–179. Boston: Allyn and Bacon, Inc.

Pedersen, P.
1979   Non-Western psychology: the search for alternatives. In *Perspectives on Cross-Cultural Psychology*, ed. A. Marsella, R. Tharp, and T. Ciborowski, 77–98. New York: Academic Press.

1981   Alternative futures for cross-cultural counseling and psychotherapy. In *Cross-Cultural Counseling and Psychotherapy*, ed. A. Marsella and P. Pedersen, 312–337. New York: Pergamon Press.

President's Commission on Mental Health
1978   Task panel reports, vols. 2, 3, and appendix. Washington, D.C.: Superintendent of Documents.

Prince, R.
1980   Variations in psychotherapeutic procedures. In *Handbook of Cross-Cultural Psychology*, ed. H. Triandis and J. Draguns, 6:291–349. Boston: Allyn and Bacon, Inc.

Pukui, M., S. Elbert, and E. Mookini
1975   *The Pocket Hawaiian Dictionary*. Honolulu: University Press of Hawaii.

Pukui, M., E. Haertig, and C. Lee
1972   *Nānā I Ke Kumu*, vol. 1. Honolulu: Hui Hānai.

Pukui, M., E. Haertig, C. Lee, and J. McDermott
1979   *Nānā I Ke Kumu*, vol. 2. Honolulu: Hui Hānai.

Redhorse, J.
1980   American Indian elders: unifiers of Indian families. *Social Casework* 61 (October): 490–493.

Reusch, J.
1967   The role of communication in therapeutic transactions. In *The Human Dialogue,* ed. A. Montague and F. Matson, 260–266. New York: The Free Press.

Reusch, J., and G. Bateson
1951   *Communication: The Social Matrix of Psychiatry.* New York: W. W. Norton and Company.

Reynolds, D., and C. Keifer
1977   Cultural adaptability as an attribute of therapies: the case of Morita psychotherapy. *Culture, Medicine and Psychiatry* 1:395–412.

Richardson, E.
1981   Cultural and historical perspectives in counseling American Indians. In *Counseling the Culturally Different,* ed. D. W. Sue, 216–255. New York: John Wiley and Sons.

Ritchie, J.
1976   Cultural time out: generalized therapeutic sociocultural mechanisms among the Maori. In *Culture-Bound Syndromes, Ethnopsychiatry and Alternate Therapies,* ed. W. Lebra, 201–210. Honolulu: University Press of Hawaii.

Rogers, E., and F. Shoemaker
1971   *Communication of Innovations: A Cross-Cultural Approach.* New York: The Free Press.

Ruiz, R.
1981   Cultural and historical perspectives in counseling Hispanics. In *Counseling the Culturally Different,* ed. D. W. Sue, 186–215. New York: John Wiley and Sons.

Ruiz, R., and A. Padilla
1979   Counseling Latinos. In *Counseling American Minorities,* eds. D. Atkinson, G. Morten, and D. W. Sue, 169–190. Dubuque, Iowa: Wm. C. Brown Company.

Scheflen, A.
1973   *Communicational Structure: Analysis of a Psychotherapy Transaction.* Bloomington: Indiana University Press.

Shook, E. V.
1983   Ho'oponopono: a discussion guide for two videotapes. Honolulu: University of Hawaii School of Social Work and Pacific Basin Family and Child Center. (An educational publication for limited distribution.)

Simonson, D.
1981   *Pidgin To Da Max.* Honolulu: Peppovision, Inc.

1982   *Pidgin To Da Max Hanahou.* Honolulu: Peppovision, Inc.

Smith, E.
1981   Cultural and historical perspectives in counseling blacks. In *Counseling the Culturally Different,* ed. D. W. Sue, 141–185. New York: John Wiley and Sons.

Speck, R., and V. Rueveni
1969   Network therapy—a developing concept. *Family Process* 8:182–191.

Spradley, J., and D. McCurdy
   1972   *The Cultural Experience: Ethnography in a Complex Society.* Chicago: Science Research Associates.

Sue, D. W.
   1981   *Counseling the Culturally Different.* New York: John Wiley and Sons.

Sue, D. W., and S. Sue
   1977   Barriers to effective cross-cultural counseling. *Journal of Counseling Psychology* 24:420–429.

   1979   Counseling Chinese-Americans. In *Counseling American Minorities,* ed. D. Atkinson, G. Morten, and D. W. Sue, 85–112. Dubuque, Iowa: Wm. C. Brown Company.

Sue, S.
   1978   Toward a strategy of primary prevention. Paper presented at a meeting of the Western Psychological Association, San Francisco, California.

Sue, S., and H. McKinney
   1975   Asian Americans in the community mental health care system. *American Journal of Orthopsychiatry* 45 (1): 111–118.

Sundberg, N.
   1981   Research and research hypotheses about effectiveness in intercultural counseling. In *Counseling Across Cultures,* ed. P. Pedersen, J. Draguns, W. Lonner, and J. Trimble, 304–342. Honolulu: University Press of Hawaii.

Torrey, E.
   1972   *The Mind Game: Witchdoctors and Psychiatrists.* New York: Emerson Hall Publishers, Inc.

Trimble, J.
   1976   Value differences among American Indians: concerns for the concerned counselor. In *Counseling Across Cultures,* ed. P. Pedersen, J. Draguns, W. Lonner, and J. Trimble, 65–81. Honolulu: University Press of Hawaii.

Truax, C., and R. Carkuff
   1967   *Toward Effective Counseling and Psychotherapy: Training and Practice.* Chicago: Aldine Publishing Company.

Tseng, W., and J. Hsu
   1979   Culture and psychotherapy. In *Perspectives on Cross-Cultural Psychology,* ed. A. Marsella, R. Tharp, and T. Ciborowski, 333–345. New York: Academic Press.

Tseng, W., and J. McDermott
   1975   Psychotherapy: historical roots, universal elements and cultural variations. *American Journal of Psychiatry* 132 (4): 378–384.

   1981   *Culture, Mind and Therapy.* New York: Brunner/Mazel Publishers.

Tylor, E.
   1874   *Primitive Culture.* New York.

Wallace, A.
   1970   *Culture and Personality,* 2nd ed. New York: Random House.

Weidman, H.
  1973   Implications of the culture broker concept for the delivery of health
          care. Paper presented at the annual meeting of the Southern Anthro-
          pological Society, Wrightsville Beach, North Carolina.

Young, B.
  1980   The Hawaiians. In *Peoples and Cultures of Hawaii: A Psychocultural
          Profile*, ed. J. McDermott, W. Tseng, and T. Maretzki, 5–24. Hono-
          lulu: University Press of Hawaii.

Youngman, G., and M. Sadongnei
  1979   Counseling the American Indian child. In *Counseling American
          Minorities*, ed. D. Atkinson, G. Morten, and D. W. Sue, 59–62.
          Dubuque, Iowa: Wm. C. Brown Company.

Index